YORK N

General Editors: Pr
of Stirling) & Profe
University of Beirut

Thomas Hardy

THE TRUMPET-MAJOR

Notes by Margaret Stonyk

BA (ADELAIDE) PH D (LEEDS)

LONGMAN
YORK PRESS

YORK PRESS
Immeuble Esseily, Place Riad Solh, Beirut.

LONGMAN GROUP LIMITED
Longman House, Burnt Mill
Harlow, Essex CM20 2JE, England

First published 1980
Reprinted 1985
ISBN 0 582 78202 3
Produced by Longman Group (FE) Ltd
Printed in Hong Kong

Contents

Part 1

Introduction

The life of Thomas Hardy

Thomas Hardy was born in south-west England in 1840, in the small Dorsetshire village of Bockhampton. His family's modest, indeed peasant, origins were to haunt Hardy throughout his life, and all his novels develop a theme of class barriers restricting the growth of personality and mutilating natural emotions. One of the ironies of his achievement as a writer is the contrast between his sympathetic interpretation of the life of the ignorant countryman, and his ruthless rejection of his actual relatives in the country. By modern standards of judgement, Hardy had much to be proud of in his immediate family, since they had risen in the space of two generations from paupers, servants and casual labourers to a mason owning his own business (Hardy's father) and the headmistress of a girls' school (his cousin Tryphena). This was certainly proof of hard work and ambition. A writer like the Scottish Thomas Carlyle (1795–1881) was able to take pride in the obscurity of his 'peasant' birth as he called it, since it made his intellectual achievements all the greater; however the south-west of England was a deeply conservative and class-conscious society without a tradition of self-sufficiency, and Hardy felt only embarrassment and shame at his humble beginnings. He concentrated in later life on a private and fanciful belief that the Hardys were a remnant of an ancient land-owning family; sadly, the sort of pointless self-deception that brought about the ruin of his heroine in *Tess of the D'Urbervilles* (1891). Curiously, Hardy the novelist is always clear-sighted about those facts of love, snobbery and self-delusion that brought him as much grief in private life as they did his characters.

Hardy had an ambitious mother who provided him with books and saw to it that he was educated beyond the usual reach of a country child of obscure family; here she was helped by a charitably-inclined aristocratic woman who took a special fancy to Thomas and gave him his lifelong taste for 'noble dames' forever out of the aspiring hero's reach. At the age of nine, Thomas went to a school where the curriculum imitated the education of the sons of gentlemen, and he learned Latin and French. His life was already divided between ambition for the life of a gentleman with a profession, probably as a clergyman, and a real enjoyment of folk traditions as he played the fiddle with his father at uninhibited local entertainments. At the age of sixteen Hardy left school after an unusually prolonged education for a boy of his background, and was articled as a pupil to an architect in Dorchester. He was assured of a respectable and comfortable livelihood, although an architect was at that time considered not a gentleman but a tradesman, and Hardy still hoped to go to university. He continued a course of wide and erratic reading to supplement his education so far, and got up every morning at five o'clock to study Greek which was then a requirement for university entrance. The son of a local clergyman introduced Hardy to modern thought, including the doubts that were being cast by modern science and philosophy on certain aspects of Christianity, and these discoveries were to shape the novelist's view of the world ruled over by a pitiless Nature. The subsequent death of his friend by suicide further darkened Hardy's naturally pessimistic outlook.

In 1862 Hardy left his original firm and went up to London to work for the architect Arthur Blomfield. There is some evidence that he applied to enter the University of Cambridge as a student, and was rejected as under-prepared. During his stay in London he gained a much wider experience of life and lost his earlier desire to be ordained as a minister of the Church of England. Hardy ceased to be a believing Christian, though he retained to the end of his life a keen if somewhat illogical interest in church architecture, sermons and politics.

The ambition to be a writer, and preferably a poet, replaced the old desire to preach. When Hardy's health broke down, he returned in 1867 to his original firm in Dorset, where he lived in his mother's house, worked on church restoration, and began his first novel, *The Poor Man and the Lady*. The work was subsequently destroyed by Hardy after it had been soundly criticised by various readers including the established novelist George Meredith (1828–1909), who nevertheless saw that this violent and inept satire on aristocratic society showed promise and advised Hardy to try again. The tone of this first novel had been misjudged, but the theme pointed to Hardy's lifelong preoccupation with social class and sexual passion.

In 1870 Hardy was writing the first of his novels to be published, *Desperate Remedies*, and continuing his work as an architect. While he was restoring a church in a Cornish village, he met his future wife, Emma Gifford, and after a four-year courtship (quite usual in the nineteenth century and before among people rich enough to be prudent, as a character in *The Trumpet-Major* testifies), the by no means young lovers were married. Hardy had found Emma pleasantly sympathetic towards his ambition to establish himself as a writer, but the relationship soon soured; Emma came to object to Hardy's low birth, his bohemian friends, agnosticism, contempt for her own efforts at writing, embarrassing and hurtful jibes at marriage, and general neglect of her. Hardy appears to have grown disenchanted with his marriage very rapidly, and showed a cold impatience with his demanding wife. Despite his private unhappiness he was writing fluently and with increasing success novels which appeared first as serials and then in volume form. *Under the Greenwood Tree* (1872), *Far From the Madding Crowd* (1874), *The Return of the Native* (1878), *The Trumpet-Major* (1880), *The Mayor of Casterbridge* (1886), *The Woodlanders* (1887), *Tess of the D'Urbervilles* (1891) and *Jude the Obscure* (1896) are merely the most notable titles from a lengthy list of novels and stories, some experimental, some melodramatic, two (including *The Trumpet-Major*) relatively kindly portraits of rural life, but all darkening into the painfully tragic vision of the last and probably the greatest of his novels, *Tess* and *Jude*.

By 1885 the money the success of his novels had brought him enabled Hardy to build a large, notoriously ugly and uncomfortable house in Dorchester, not far from his birthplace. Dorset, or 'Wessex' as he called it, became the permanent setting for his fictions. When *Tess of the D'Urbervilles*, a bitter story of a country girl ruined by her aristocratic seducer, the blind hypocrisy of her husband and the casual cruelty of nature, and *Jude the Obscure*, the even darker tale of how a peasant boy's search for education and sexual fulfilment brings him to destruction, caused scandals by their outspokenness and pessimistic philosophy, Hardy ceased to write novels. He may have been disgusted and depressed by the fury of his critics, or, more probably, he may have felt that he had taken the novel form to its limits so far as his own art was concerned. After 1896 he turned to poetry, and his gifts as a lyrical poet expressing the private negative emotions of disappointment and grief make the achievement of these later years quite as remarkable as the long list of fine novels.

Emma Hardy died in 1912, and Hardy remarried two years later, though this second match was ironically destroyed by his bizarre obsession with the memory of his dead wife as he had known her during their courtship. While he never achieved happiness in his private life, he was greatly respected as an active man of letters. He received numbers of writers and admirers until his death in 1928, when the vastness of his reputation as a poet and philosopher outweighed his status as an unbeliever, for he was buried in Westminster Abbey among the greatest writers of his nation, while his heart, symbolically, was returned to a grave in Dorset.

Hardy had made one attempt to create a master-work which would sum up his preoccupations: *The Dynasts* (1903–8) is an epic-drama of the Napoleonic period which at present appeals only to a minority of readers and has never caught the popular taste. Despite the setting, it does not bear the relationship to *The Trumpet-Major* that we expect, except in some isolated panoramic effects. Hardy's greatest achievements are found elsewhere, in the uncompromising bleakness of the later novels, and in the poetry of private grief and despair which seeks to understand and evaluate rather than merely to indulge feelings of desolation and loss.

Hardy's life was not, so far as we can tell, a happy one, though in outward terms it was buoyantly successful. He was handicapped in his own view by his humble background, and suffered as a young man and throughout his two marriages from a sense of frustration in love. Though he is reticent about such matters, his poems suggest that his first wife was not his original choice, that she had reason to be jealous of other women, and that Hardy had the misfortune, after resenting her throughout their long married life, to fall in love with her memory after she had died. His second marriage was, not surprisingly, a failure. Most of his novels deal with this theme of sexual pessimism, of frustrated or despised love or love that comes too late, and the impossibility of getting an irrational passion to conform to his century's strict laws controlling marriage. In *The Trumpet-Major* the comic contrasting of Anne the virtuous heroine and Matilda the half-reformed prostitute shows the typical conflict between the ideal and the real forms of love in a lighthearted fashion, and the pretty caprices of Anne and the perplexed gallantry of her suitors still contain a suggestion of the private bitterness out of which this delicate comedy was born. Similarly, the miserliness of old Derriman, which Hardy criticises so pungently in *The Trumpet-Major*, echoes in a strange way Hardy's own much-discussed meanness and fascination with legacies. In real life, the poverty out of which he had sprung prevented him from enjoying the pleasures of generosity and small daily luxuries, even after his industry as a novelist had made him rich.

The influence of Hardy's life upon his novels

Hardy's novels and poetry show us a writer who was instinctive rather than philosophic, and who exaggerated his peculiar insights so as to make his readers look questioningly at the natural and social worlds they inhabited. His writings cannot be seen merely as illustrations of social change in the nineteenth century, but as universal statements of the human condition which Hardy saw alternately as grimly comic or purely tragic. The novels frequently call to mind Shakespeare, the greatest of English writers, in their plots, language and direct quotation; at his best, Hardy shares Shakespeare's imaginative vitality and common sense. Hardy is also a Romantic in the precise sense of the word; a poet who believes that man is only at peace with himself when he is in harmony with the natural world, which in its unspoiled state is the best of teachers, and that the English language at its purest is heard in the speech of uncorrupted country people.

Hardy believed that it was his duty to present a personal, even idiosyncratic vision of the triangular relationship between man, nature and society. Other novelists tried to smooth out the inconsistent and irrational to present a fictional world which would appear probable to the average reader, but Hardy dealt magnificently with the uncommon. His novels, even this relatively orthodox one, are full of coincidences, bizarre events, unnatural eavesdroppings, and above all a tendency to record the tricks of perception played by the individual eye: in *The Trumpet-Major* the tall and gangling John appears to the galloping Anne as a wayside cross, and passing objects flash 'like strokes' before her terrified, half-shut eyes.

The Trumpet-Major gives us a powerful sense of Hardy's extraordinary sense of the past shaping or distorting human lives. His biographies suggest that he felt his whole life to have been warped by the circumstances of his background and his early disappointments in love, and he was convinced that he was doomed to repeat certain actions and to give up hope for the future in his obsession with the past. Hardy had been deeply impressed as a young child on hearing his grandmother remark that a hot, thundery summer was like the one they had had in the year of the French Revolution, and the simple parish scandal of the dismissal of the church musicians in favour of a new organ touched him just as keenly. In *The Trumpet-Major* Hardy exhibits his sense of history, showing the greatness of little events and the ordinariness of great ones; rural history is not a comically diminished equivalent to Napoleon's dreams of European conquest, but something that touches and changes individual lives. Indeed, if we are responsive to the symbolism of the novel, we find that the pikes of the countrymen stored in the church as a rough defence against the French attack have a longer existence when transformed into the walking sticks and garden tools of peacetime than have the grand armies and warships of international conflict. These visible relics, Hardy argues, interpret the past age to a new generation, and the Preface he added to the novel in 1912 elaborates this point.

It is well known that Hardy used the geographical setting of his own early life to create an alternative world that remains constant throughout his novels and poetry: the fictional 'Wessex' that is now better known around the world than the original Dorset. He changed the place names in order to assimilate the country as his own imaginative property, and the foreign student in particular need not feel obliged to compare and contrast the maps of Dorset and 'Wessex'. Dorset and its history gave Hardy what he needed for his characters; the extra dimension of a history in which they could take their places as the latest generation. All his novels insist on our need to feel that we belong to a continuing chain of life. The local and universal history that Hardy conjures up is rarely happy and often grisly, but he assures us that no emotion that has been felt is quite lost to memory, and we feel either the consolation or the oppressive weight of the countless lives preceding our own.

A note on the text

Hardy began by collecting Napoleonic material in 1877, and two years later in February 1879 submitted an outline of a novel to Leslie Stephen, editor of the *Cornhill Magazine*. Stephen demurred: historical novels were rarely popular as serials, and Hardy offered the projected work to Dr Donald Macleod, a pious Presbyterian clergyman who was editing *Good Words*. The work had been conceived as a three-volume novel, in which form it would eventually be published, and some alterations were necessary to turn it into twelve monthly instalments. Not only did small adjustments of plot have to be made, heightening suspense and hinting at future complications, but the tastes of a very conservative readership had to be taken into account. Matilda's past could only be hinted at vaguely, Mrs Garland's character became less pronounced, the embraces of the lovers were forbidden by the editor, all mildly profane language was dropped, and the famous passage satirising an English Sunday had to be altered so that Bob waited for his bride on a Saturday. Hardy liked, he said, to be accounted 'a good hand at a serial' and they brought him money; he was used to expurgating his text in order to suit the policy of a family magazine, because the cuts could be restored in volume publication. *The Trumpet-Major* was serialised between January and December 1880, and the revised version of the serial text came out in volume form in October 1880. Hardy saw three editions of his novel through the press in 1880, 1895 and 1912. A Preface, reprinted in most current editions, was added in 1912. The best modern edition is the New Wessex Edition of *The Trumpet-Major*, edited by Barbara Hardy, Macmillan, London, 1974. See Part 5, Suggestions for further reading, p.67.

Part 2

Summaries
of THE TRUMPET-MAJOR

A general summary

The Trumpet-Major is set early in the first decade of the nineteenth
century, and its hero is one of three suitors for the hand of Anne
Garland, a pretty but obscure girl living in a country village. John
Loveday is honourable, sensitive and Anne's obvious choice, but she
cannot love him as he asks and has set her heart on the fickle Bob, his
brother, who pursues one woman after another but always comes back
to Anne. At times she is tempted out of snobbery to accept Festus
Derriman, the stupid and boastful local squire, who is likely to inherit his
miserly old uncle's considerable riches. Despite the alarms of a
threatened invasion by Napoleon's troops and the battle of Trafalgar in
which Bob takes part, the story avoids violent action and concentrates
on private emotions. John finally gives up a prospering courtship of
Anne for the sake of his brother's happiness and because he knows she
loves the careless younger man, and goes out to die on the battlefields of
Spain.

Detailed summaries

Chapter 1: What was seen from the Window overlooking the Down

Mrs Garland, the widow of a landscape painter, and her daughter Anne
live as tenants of Miller Loveday at Overcombe Mill near Budmouth at
the time of the Napoleonic Wars. Their placid lives are interrupted by a
'fine sight' of massed soldiers come to make camp on the downs in
preparation for a defence against invasion.

NOTES AND GLOSSARY:
Hardy seems to promise nothing more than a picturesque tale of bygone
days in rural England, and his first chapter opens on a sleepy noonday
scene. But the portrait of Anne shows how the tale is to involve the moral
and emotional education of this outwardly conventional young girl, and
it begins the demonstration of how all that Hardy finds admirable in
human character is closely linked to the world of nature. Anne, sewing
her carpet at her window, becomes for a moment all those ladies of
romance who waited patiently for a knight to come and carry them
away, and the image suggests the fairytale aspect of this story of

charmed lives. The mood of the chapter changes from indolence to exertion as we watch the miniature history of the characters begin, and the gentle past of Overcombe is comically speeded up in the mushroom rise of the tent city.

stopped diapason: a soft, muffled note on the organ
bolting: separating bran from the flour
hopper: a mechanism for feeding grain to the mill machinery
beacon: a system of bonfires organised along the south coast to give warning of an attack by the French troops

Chapter 2: Somebody knocks and comes in

Overcombe Mill, part factory, part private house, and the decent, hard-working Lovedays are described. The Miller is 'hale through and through' with a soldier son John and a sailor son Bob who is expected to give up the sea and become a miller himself. Anne and her mother are invited to a 'randy' or musical supper to welcome John from the camp.

NOTES AND GLOSSARY:
Setting matters as much as character in this novel, and Hardy is laying the foundations of Anne's eventual decision to marry Bob and stay within the world she knows, paying tribute to the power of memory and the claims of family affection. She learns about the workings of the Mill as she discovers Bob's qualities and her own feelings, and the dual nature of the building, public and private, suggests the balance characters in the novel have to maintain between their personal feelings and the claims of society. The Mill shows how time may be partially resisted by industry and inherited duties, and the central symbol of the weathervane predicts ominously that Bob will supplant John in Anne's affections even though the two brothers are here literally 'one and the same'. The welcoming of the 'soldiers' wives' by Anne and her mother emphasises the innocence of the Overcombe ladies and prepares us for the equally gorgeous and immoral Matilda later. The chapter closes with the superb set-piece describing the changeful, human scene of the camp, the church-tower, symbol of a more permanent community, and the eternal stars shining above.

Gothic: a jocularly vague word referring to the Dark and Middle Ages, *c*.1000 to 1500 AD
ceorls or villeins: low-ranking and hard-working people, certainly not 'ladies and gentlemen' as Hardy facetiously implies
hips instead of gables: the Mill sprawls in an unfashionable way instead of rising tall like a Victorian house

mampus:	(*dialect*) crowd
randy:	(*dialect*) a happy, noisy party
yeomanry:	a mounted volunteer force for which the government provided only ammunition
tattoo:	a summons for soldiers to get back to their quarters
Charles's Wain:	a country name for the constellation of stars known more generally as Ursa Major

Chapter 3: The Mill becomes an important Centre of Operations

Anne is awakened whn John Loveday supervises a party of soldiers come to water the horses in the millpond; the Miller welcomes the troop who all enjoy the fruit from his trees and the blushes of Anne. She refuses from a mixture of snobbery and modesty to go to the Miller's party, but her girlish mother is saved from disappointment when the hearty Miller comes in to carry them both off to the singing and dancing, and Anne and John meet consciously for the first time since childhood.

NOTES AND GLOSSARY:
Hardy contrasts the unthinking pleasure of the soldiers as they enjoy the fruit and the sight of Anne's beauty with his author's awareness of their mortality and the general disappointment which accompanies experience, without lessening our pleasure as readers in the warmth and charm of the scene. The novel concentrates almost exclusively on attractive subjects and characters, but is not truly optimistic. Anne's refusal to join the party shows the negative side of her nature.

mill-tail:	the passage through which water races from the mill-wheel
picters:	an unlearned form of 'pictures'
maidy Anne:	a country form of address for unmarried girls

Chapter 4: Who were present at the Miller's little Entertainment

Hardy concentrates on the minor figures at the party, the foreign soldiers and the ancient veterans wounded in long-forgotten battles, and the humble village volunteers. Anne, embarrassed by the frank admiration of the soldiers, has to seek out the village folk she usually ignores.

NOTES AND GLOSSARY:
The deliberately slow progress of this chapter gives John's admiration for Anne time to grow into something stronger, while Hardy mildly reprimands the heroine for her exclusiveness and places the present war, seen at this stage only in terms of glamorous uniforms and chivalrous language, in the ironic and grisly context of the veterans' shattered limbs

and hazy recollections. Anne will redeem her haughtiness here in the later chapter set at Portland Beal, when she accepts the telescope and conversation of an old sailor as she watches Bob's ship disappear. Her emotions will by then have been deepened by an acquaintance with personal suffering she does not have now.

toss-potting:	heavy drinking
chiel:	country form of 'child'
Valenciennes:	a French town besieged by the English early in the Revolutionary Wars that preceded the war against Napoleon
morticed:	a carpentry term for joining two pieces by a projecting tongue
wownd:	local pronunciation of 'wound'
pummy:	(*dialect*) pulp, originally made from cider-apples

Chapter 5: The Song and the Stranger

John is captivated by Anne's charm and she uses her renewed acquaintance with him to ask after Bob the sailor. John says Bob is in love, and Anne hopes secretly that she is the lady. Songs and dances are interrupted by Festus Derriman, the hulking local squire and cavalry officer, who is flushed with liquor and falls impulsively in love with Anne.

NOTES AND GLOSSARY:
Hardy's description of the Miller's party gives us our understanding of the author's approval of the virtue of hospitality in the world of the novel; by this generous behaviour characters create memories and establish friendships which compensate them for the brevity of their lives. If the fear of invasion, so real to the villagers, is not shared by his readers, Hardy balances this with a poignant sense of individual tragedy, as in the case of the recruiting officer Stanner who appears throughout the novel and who, we are told, is to die in Spain 'a few years after this pleasantly-spent summer'. The villagers' acceptance of the bullying, boastful Festus may seem too docile, but they prove to be right. The Miller's reproof to John: "Tis as well to be neighbourly with folks, if they be not quite onbearable', is a dignified statement of the generous views of Overcombe and an admission that Festus is no threat to anyone.

the Farnese Hercules:	a larger than life-size statue of the muscular demi-god stood in the Farnese Palace in Rome
spud:	a small tool for digging out weeds
barton:	farmyard
Dutch cabbage:	a red cabbage
Rufus:	a Latin scholar's word for a red-haired man

Chapter 6: Old Mr Derriman of Oxwell Hall

Anne goes as usual to collect a newspaper from Benjamin Derriman, the miserly and lowborn owner of the decayed Oxwell Hall, and as she sits reading to him Festus arrives to torment his uncle into offering him lodgings and making him his heir. Cripplestraw, the malicious servant, freezes Festus's blood with tales of death in battle, while old Derriman hopes that his favourite Anne will marry Festus.

NOTES AND GLOSSARY:
Hardy shows the effects of time upon men and objects. Oxwell Hall is the reverse of the Mill; no longer a symbol of community order, since the original line of owners has died out, it is in the hands of a former servant and has fallen into decay, the natural world reclaiming its stone and metal. The health and generosity of the Miller is changed into the meanness of the more dead than alive Derriman who has cut himself off from any tie which could involve a claim on his fortune. The fate of the newspaper Anne collects shows how the great news of the nation is gradually passed down the social ladder until it wraps the bread and cheese of the grinder's boy; a servant, Hardy implies, may live as useful and inwardly gratifying a life as the greatest in the land.

gnomon: the fixed pin of a sundial; its shadow indicates the time of day
Duty of Man: a popular devotional manual of the period
lamiger: a lame or crippled person
sniche: (*dialect*) grasping, greedy

Chapter 7: How they talked in the Pastures

Anne cannot resist leading Festus on to show the full extent of his stupidity and cowardice. But her initial amusement and lurking sympathy for him soon change to irritation, and she leaves him abruptly.

NOTES AND GLOSSARY:
We become aware of hidden depths in Anne's outwardly demure character; she plays on Festus's vanity and ignorance just as the servant had. Even if, as most critics agree, Hardy failed by accident or design to create a fully believable villain in Festus, the effect he has on the more realistically portrayed Anne is always absorbing. He leads her first to an awareness of her power over men and then to a consciousness of her passionate nature when she escapes from him in Chapter 28.

giltycups: a local name for buttercups, vivid yellow field-flowers
besom: broom

Chapter 8: Anne makes a Circuit of the Camp

A villager, Granny Seamore, congratulates Anne on her new sweetheart while Hardy ironically provides his own description of how Festus's ill nature has remained unchanged from childhood. Festus is now obsessed with Anne and cannot understand that her modesty is genuine. Anne tolerates him out of curiosity, though her fear of his temper makes her keep out of his way; her ambitious mother thinks she is avoiding John Loveday, and is satisfied.

NOTES AND GLOSSARY:
We notice as the character of Festus is explored in a long digression by Hardy that all the main characters are recollected as children, and that none of them have altered much since then. Hardy believed in all his novels that character is usually inherited or at least fixed early by physical surroundings and influences, and his biographical writings show he knew it to be true in his case. There is an additional suggestion that the central trio have not lost the simplicity and guilelessness romantically attributed to children.

the Collect and Gospel:	the prayer-book and the Bible
zeed:	the unlearned form of 'saw'
put on the big pot:	to behave with false importance, to brag
ipso facto:	(*Latin*) by that fact
in his cups:	when drunk
Old Nick:	a folk name for the devil; it was supposed to be bad luck to refer to him outright
sutlers:	small provision-sellers who followed the army
heir-presumptive:	the likely inheritor of old Derriman's money. Usually used to refer to crowns and thrones, and thus it mocks Festus's comparatively modest expectations

Chapter 9: Anne is kindly fetched by the Trumpet-Major

Old Derriman goes on an unheard-of expensive holiday to Budmouth to recover from his encounters with Festus, who seems bent on frightening the old man to death. John Loveday fears that Anne is encouraging Festus, and when she is kept late at a party in a neighbouring village he decides to fetch her home and discover her true feelings on the way. By ill luck, just as Anne is responding to John's enthusiastic talk of his military life and his music, they pass Oxwell Hall where Festus is holding a rowdy drinking party for his soldier friends; she suspects wrongly that John has arranged the walk to demonstrate Festus's bad character. The situation is further complicated when old Derriman comes home unexpectedly.

To prevent a quarrel, Anne insists that both John and Festus accompany her home, but ends by running off alone when John refuses to give his drunken rival the slip. Festus ends up cheated by Anne and locked out of the Hall by his cunning uncle.

NOTES AND GLOSSARY:
Hardy touches on aspects of rural life which give the novel its immediate and lasting charm: the Miller's compulsive hospitality, and the christening-party which suggests not only life going on and constantly renewing itself, but being a very pleasant thing taken all round. Anne is given Hardy's approval for recognising John's 'single-minded ingenuousness'; we must be careful not to credit him with more insight and intellect than he really possesses. Like all the admirable characters in the novel, he has firm moral principles and a proven capacity for feeling without active intelligence of a bookish sort. The scene at Oxwell Hall is a deliberately staged counter to the kindly and dignified hospitality at the Mill in Chapters 3, 4 and 5; the Miller's party had symbolised community harmony, whereas Festus only heads a drunken rabble.

watering-place:	a seaside resort or inland spa. Budmouth has both sea bathing, then undertaken for health rather than pleasure, and sulphurous springs
christening-party:	a celebration to mark the baptism of a baby
eltrot:	a local name for cow-parsley, a tall weed
serpent:	an obsolete coiled wind-instrument
twenties:	cheap candles sold at twenty to the pound
rummers:	large drinking glasses
tear-brass set:	a rowdy or boisterous crowd
scram blue-vinnied gallicrow:	(*dialect*) feeble, mouldy old scarecrow
knap:	hill-top

Chapter 10: The Match-making Virtues of a Double Garden

Anne is filled with a 'sense of her own loneliness' as she watches the soldiers court the local girls, but her pride and her dislike of Festus keep her in the Mill garden. She talks with John Loveday and grows interested in him 'as a brother', and her mother, now anticipating her own marriage to the Miller, allows the friendship to take its course, feeling great satisfaction when Anne slights Festus on a tour of the camp.

NOTES AND GLOSSARY:
Hardy takes advantage of a natural pause in his narrative to draw the links between Anne and the world of nature still closer, and so recommend her character to us. The Mill, though picturesque, is not unrealistically perfect, and Hardy dwells with mild ironic pleasure on the

insects spoiling a garden which is otherwise an earthly paradise. Anne
and John meet in a garden like the lovers in innumerable romantic tales,
though their own love story is to be an incomplete one. For a moment
the charmed atmosphere of the Mill and the emotional exploration of
the lovers have us so enthralled that we lose our sense of a wider world;
the figures going up to the camp are 'like bees'.

the land of Lot: the plain of Jordan in the Bible; see Genesis 13:10

Chapter 11: Our People are affected by the Presence of Royalty

Miller Loveday has hastened his proposal to improve John's chances
with Anne, but she feels only disgust at her mother's willingness to sink
in the social scale. Once more she thinks of the lordly Festus, and refuses
to join a family party to go and see the King pass on the high road on his
way to Budmouth. When Festus comes to harass her as soon as the
others have left, she runs to catch them up, and John, having asked Mrs
Garland's formal permission, proposes marriage to Anne. She refuses
him, as she has no ambition to be the wife of a merely 'respectable' man
and live in barracks. Mrs Garland finally accepts the Miller, the 'dusty
old leather coaches' rattle past, and Anne is dreaming of Festus again.

NOTES AND GLOSSARY:
This chapter helps us to understand Hardy's imaginative egalitarianism;
his feeling that the inner lives of all his characters are to be taken
seriously. Though the villagers are disappointed by the humble appearance of the royal coaches, Hardy is in a mood to appreciate the
unpretentious nature of the King, whom he chooses to see not as a
pathetic, intermittently insane figurehead, but as a man of 'bucolic
tastes' like the Miller. The Miller himself, in the first paragraph, 'loved
his son as much as any miller or private gentleman could do'; rank does
not alter the quality of the feeling. If we have tended to patronise the
unintellectual and unreflective characters so far, we are taken aback by
Anne's sensitive response to her mother's proposed marriage: 'To wake
into cold daylight like this, when and because her mother had gone into
the land of romance, was dreadful and new to her, and like an increase of
years without living them.' We may have been amused by John's prosaic
talk of rank and barracks when he proposed so unsuccessfully, but
Hardy challenges our tendency to under-estimate his characters in the
image of the rising sun which causes John to 'blaze in the rays like a very
god of war' and bathes Anne in a similarly supernatural radiance. The
instinctive closeness to nature of these people, and the intensity with
which they live out the modest range of experience available to them,
turn them into dignified symbols of men and women of every period and
social class.

cortège: a formal procession of vehicles

Chapter 12: How Everybody, great and small, climbed to the Top of the Downs

---

Budmouth is now a fashionable resort for the aristocracy and a review of the troops is planned on the downs above Overcombe. Anne sees both Festus and John on parade, while Bob Loveday, now home from the sea, watches the same scene from another part of the crowd. The Miller hears that a letter is waiting for him at Budmouth and John sets out on foot to fetch it while Anne is driven by the family servant to see the town.

NOTES AND GLOSSARY:
In this chapter Hardy again plays with the notion of relative scale; the coaches of the aristocracy creep in the distance along the highway like ants upon an ant-walk. For once we are made to stand back and survey South Wessex from a distant vantage-point instead of concentrating on the sheltered Mill. Our point of view is altered still further by having the central male characters reduced to mere dots in 'the concrete, straight lines of red and blue', their capacities for thinking and feeling blotted out by the distant prospect and the military drill. Bob Loveday is introduced in a passage out of character with his later development by the author; for a moment we see into his innermost thoughts and he never again displays such imagination. Hardy ends the set-piece of the military review with a solemn variation of his constant theme of *ubi sunt* ('where are they now?'); how the gallantry and colour of the scene have resolved themselves into scattered handfuls of grave-dust. But only he thinks of this; his characters disregard the flight of time and go on with their small preoccupations.

monument: by Hardy's day there was a monument to Admiral
                            Hardy (seen in Chapter 33) north-east of Portisham
King Jarge: the local pronunciation of 'King George'

Chapter 13: The Conversation in the Crowd

John shows Anne the sights of the resort, and she is pleased with the 'poetical', 'educated', 'well-mannered' and 'tender' qualities of the man she has rejected. She picks up a flower thrown at her by the lovesick Festus and impulsively offers it to John, realising guiltily that this caprice may provoke a serious quarrel. John discovers from the letter that Bob is coming home to be married, and Anne feigns indifference.

NOTES AND GLOSSARY:
This scene will contrast with Anne's later visit to Budmouth with the less intelligent Bob dressed in his provincial finery. Hardy manages a good

deal of indirect criticism of Anne in his detailed description of her dress and her assessment of John's effect upon the crowd, which reads like a summary of her private thought. Yet her vanity is so uncomplicated and her conviction that she ought not marry John so right that she is not censured. Even her flirtatious play with the flower is the instinctive action of a Hardy heroine whose setting of lover against lover is done less out of mischief than as an attempt to dramatise and sort out conflicts in her own nature. Her desire to save the flower from destruction has a symbolic significance, as though at some level she is aware of the loss of all that is lovely, including herself, in the rapid flight of time.

First Consul: a title offered to Bonaparte in 1799 by the French Republic which modelled itself on ancient Rome

Chapter 14: Later in the Evening of the same Day

The family and neighbours gather to hear Bob's news of his forthcoming marriage to a Miss Matilda Johnson after a mere two weeks' courtship. While the Miller is distracted by his misgivings, old Derriman arrives with his precious 'box' which he wants hidden in case of an invasion by the French. The villagers go outside to wait for Bob, and Anne secretly burns a lock of his hair she has treasured as a keepsake.

NOTES AND GLOSSARY:
Bob's wilfulness in forgetting Anne and proposing marriage to a stranger to the family is indirectly and thoroughly criticised in the stress Hardy lays on the good fellowship of the neighbours who throng the doorway to hear the letter read. The Miller's 'I was five years a-courting my wife' adds an extra dimension to the novel, as we realise that the ageing Miller has been a young lover in his time. His opinions on any subject are worth attending to; they come reluctantly, and they always sum up the values of Hardy's rural world.

heerd ... 'nation ... 'Nater: local pronunciations of 'heard ... damnation ... Nature'
scrounch it all: a mild and meaningless oath
smit with: infatuated with
squireen: as a squire is a gentleman and landowner, Hardy lets us know what a small opinion he has of Festus's claims to gentility and wealth

Chapter 15: 'Captain' Bob Loveday, of the Merchant Service

Bob arrives at the temporarily deserted Mill and enters by an upstairs window, making himself at home by preparing a lavish feast of welcome.

He is greeted warmly and undoes his luggage for the entertainment of the neighbours, showing off monkeys, parrots and fine shawls, and giving no sign that he remembers his former attachment to Anne. When he recollects that he used to be her 'beau in a humble sort of way' she rejects his peace-offerings, and he caps his good-natured blunders that evening by disparaging Mrs Garland to the Miller.

NOTES:
Bob Loveday's considerable charm lies in his ordinariness, his luck, and that happy ability to reproduce his forebears' traits that is a partial victory over the passage of time. He may often appear foolish, but we like and admire him for his attachment to his family and their past, his unaffected relishing of the natural world, and his easy mastery of it in his sailor's training. Hardy engineers this pause in the narrative, while Bob explores his old home, to prove his hero's sensitivity to atmosphere and the tenderness of his memories. The meal he prepares is a further positive comment upon his character; though thoughtlessly free with other people's property and feelings, he is instinctively generous. The gifts he brings suggest indirectly that Bob's experience of a wider world will balance the protected character of the Mill once he becomes its master, and the handsome swearing parrot looks forward to the splendidly dressed but immoral Matilda. Bob is the first person to get the better of Anne in a dialogue, and he challenges her self-possession more dramatically than the respectful John ever could.

Chapter 16: They make Ready for the Illustrious Stranger

Mrs Garland superintends the cleaning of the Mill for the wedding, and the preparation of country delicacies on a vast scale. Bob goes into Casterbridge to meet his bride who is arriving in state on the mail-coach; after an anxious afternoon he sees her scramble from the straw of a country wagon. She is not as rich as Bob imagines her, and has spent his travelling-money on fine clothes. Her looks, Hardy tells us, are rather faded, and she seems to have been an actress.

NOTES AND GLOSSARY:
Hardy has a high regard for order and cleanliness as these are expressions of human dignity and a defence against the ravages of time. Yet as the tidy Mill is cleaned thoroughly in preparation for the wedding we see how the acts of daily living cause minute and cumulative damage to the habitation in the building-up of grease and the wearing-down of stone. The large-scale hospitality emphasises the simple generosity of Overcombe, while the scene at Casterbridge is a mild satire upon the infamous English Sunday more ruthlessly criticised by such writers as Charles Dickens (1812–70) and Samuel Butler (1835–1902). Hardy

demonstrates the resistant secular feelings of his characters, and seems willing to let the swearing of the coachman and the sermons of the parson coexist without comment. Matilda is treated rather callously by Hardy, though he will rehabilitate her later and even award her ironic view of life some praise. In a world where physical beauty, youth and simplicity are admired, Matilda is too old, too experienced and too cynical to be valued.

diachylon plaister: a medicinal compound spread thickly on a piece of cloth and applied to an inflammation of the skin
death-watches: beetles whose tapping noises sounded to the superstitious ear like coffin-nails being hammered
skitty boots: high-laced boots
barrow pig: a castrated boar
black-pot ... white-pot ... chitterlings: country delicacies of pork meats and custards
Falstaff's favourite beverage: Falstaff is a character rather like Festus, cowardly, drunken and very amusing, in Shakespeare's *Henry IV*. His favourite drink is sack, a sweet Spanish wine
bakehouses: bakeries undertook to roast Sunday joints and puddings for their patrons during the morning church service

---

Chapter 17: Two Fainting Fits and a Bewilderment

Matilda affects terror at simple country noises and sights, but the simple Overcombe folk take this as proof of good breeding. Anne and her mother are won over by the smart stranger who sets out to please them, and all goes smoothly until John arrives for tea. He and Matilda recognise each other to their mutual horror, and while she is taken upstairs to recover from a faint, John considers what must be done.

NOTES AND GLOSSARY:
Hardy gets a lot of attractively simple-minded fun out of Matilda's town-bred ways, and her experience in what were to Hardy's original readers the morally questionable worlds of actress and prostitute does not threaten to contaminate the innocence of the Garland women. The broad comedy of her first fainting fit is followed by a fine subtle dialogue as the ladies of the Mill and the actress try to take the measure of one another, and the comedy continues with the recognition scene and Bob's later cheerful candour about why he is going out to see the villagers: 'they'll like me to see 'em first on a Sunday, and in their best clothes.' As usual, Hardy uses his comic gifts to draw a fine line between ridiculous vanity and praiseworthy self-respect.

reticule:	a woman's ornamental handbag worn at this period
Pharaoh's baker:	he was dismissed in order to be hanged. See the Bible, Genesis:40

Chapter 18: The Night after the Arrival

John has a private conversation with Matilda, charging her with misconduct with several officers, and even Anne's kindness to him later that evening fails to brighten his melancholy after such an unpleasant duty. When Matilda pleads with him not to be sent away, old Derriman mistakes the couple in the garden late at night for thieves come in search of his box, and John has to pretend that he is courting an anonymous lady, whom the miser assumes is Anne. The house is awakened and the box taken away by Derriman.

NOTES AND GLOSSARY:
Matilda is the only character in the novel who can match John for intelligence and self-reliance, and it is not surprising that they become adversaries and are then suspected of a love-affair. Judged by the moral standards of the English nineteenth century, John is right to be scandalised and to turn Matilda out of the house, but Hardy himself seems to take a more tolerant attitude, since he ends by giving Matilda a respectable husband rather than punishing her with infamy. Her impulsive kindness, her constant resourcefulness, and her ability to make her own way in a world less kind than Anne's are a rebuke to John's narrow view of right and wrong. The family's singing of psalms to lively ballad tunes 'not thinking of the words' is another instance of Hardy's secularism in the novel; he is not against religion, but feels that his uncorrupted and affectionate villagers have no need of dogma to make them good.

Talleyrand:	a proverbially impassive diplomat (1754–1838) who was Napoleon's favourite minister but later secretly turned against him and secured mild terms of peace for France after the defeat of the Emperor. An interesting comparison, as Talleyrand means something to us but nothing to Matilda; as an historical personage he belongs to her future
I'll remind you of particulars:	John means that Matilda has been a camp-follower, a woman of bad character
psalms:	the Psalms of David, sung in church. were the only music permitted in pious households on the Sabbath

---

Chapter 19: Miss Johnson's Behaviour causes no little Surprise

---

Bob enlists Anne in his search for Matilda, and she is infuriated when he kisses her hand on a whim; he explains that he finds all women enchanting and has great difficulty in remaining faithful to one. John has to explain privately to his brother that Matilda is no fit wife for an honest man, but Bob goes off to find the woman he feels is good enough for him.

NOTES AND GLOSSARY:
Bob's rapid neglect of Matilda and renewed interest in Anne would strike us as not only improbable but unpleasant if Hardy did not prepare us for it by a lovingly built-up mosaic of tiny details showing how the charming and orderly life of the Mill, summed up in Anne, is working to reclaim Bob's affections. There is no fear that Matilda has committed suicide, as violent death has no place in this novel despite the wartime setting. Bob's claim that Matilda's past life makes no difference to his fondness for her calls John's rigorous sense of honour into question, even as we feel the force of his good sense and strong principles.

burr-stones:	the coarsest kind of millstone
yaw:	(nautical terminology) to go off-course
unreaves:	unravels
marline-spike:	a sharp tool for unravelling rope
grandfer:	a country form of 'grandfather'

Chapter 20: How they lessened the Effect of the Calamity

Anne begins to suspect that John has begun to court Matilda for himself after Festus tells her what his uncle saw in the garden, and she treats her former suitor with contempt for his hypocrisy. Bob comes to feel the sense of John's advice and gives up his search for Matilda, returning to the Mill to find that his father is marrying Mrs Garland at once to put the marriage preparations to good use.

NOTES AND GLOSSARY:
Festus serves once more in his principal role as tale-bearer, and Anne's curious attitude towards him is investigated; we rather admire her for the 'fear and excitement' he causes in her. Bob's return home from the search for his bride shows the mingled strength and weakness of his engaging and infuriating character; he is careless enough to toss a hugely extravagant guinea to decide his chances in matrimony, but sensible enough to draw back from this bad bargain with himself and acknowledge the 'reasonableness and good sense' of John's advice.

blue-vinnied:	mouldy
a sorry haul:	nautical slang for 'a bad job'

Chapter 21: 'Upon the Hill he turned'

The older couple are married and Bob's feast is consumed by the poor of the neighbourhood. John comes with the news that the army is moving away, and spends the last hours of his leave silently watching Anne's window. When she parts from him at the camp the next morning without ending their quarrel, Festus gloats aloud that there is now a chance for him, and Anne tells him impulsively that there is still 'one left'.

NOTES AND GLOSSARY:
The generally rosy picture of rural life so far is qualified here by mild satire in the description of the uninteresting marriage of 'middle-aged civilians'; the self-interest rather than the charity in the invitation to the poor to eat up meats which would otherwise spoil, and the general satisfaction that the snobbish widow has given up her social position to marry the Miller. This uneasy comedy throws into relief the perplexities of Anne, who is no longer her mother's fondest interest and is forced to think of her own marriage choice. As John silently bids Anne farewell, we discover one of those moments in the novel in which time seems suspended, and every insect and drop of water is caught forever, as in a painting, in the beam of light shining from her bedroom candle. But Hardy returns inexorably to his theme of time passing as the camp is struck and John rides away.

Revalley: (properly 'réveille') a call to soldiers to start the day

Chapter 22: The Two Households united

Anne has now taken her old place in Bob's affections, and she accepts his invitation to see over the Mill workings after he accidentally opens a concealed door to her apartments. She treats him with contempt although she is pleased at his infatuation, until he breaks down her reserve by making her an Aeolian harp which causes music to issue from the mill-head. Her keen delight causes the honest Bob to admit that it was John's idea, and Anne, regretting her callous treatment of her rejected lover, loses all pleasure in the instrument and has it removed.

NOTES AND GLOSSARY:
Hardy has a good deal of fun at Bob's expense here, emphasising his unsophisticated pleasures and emotional inexperience. Although his eager ordinariness will finally balance Anne's rather finicking ways, and time will elevate him socially to the rank of lieutenant, Bob is now made to seem very unpolished beside our recollection of John. The symbolic cutting through of the door signifies Bob's success in breaking down Anne's reserve, and for the first time she condescends to look at the workings of the Mill, symbolic of her own unguessed-at motives and

desires. The Aeolian harp teaches Anne that the prosaic world of air and water around her may hold a secret poetry.

ewe-lease: a meadow set aside for sheep
Aeolian harp: a stringed instrument which makes music as the wind blows through it

---

Chapter 23: Military Preparations on an Extended Scale

By the following spring the Miller has volunteered for the local militia, but Bob is too infatuated with Anne to want to go to sea in his country's defence. Mrs Loveday prompts Festus to approach Anne, but she hides from him in the Mill where Bob is able to get her promise to walk to church with him. That Sunday everything reminds Bob of his patriotic duty, and he feels that he cannot take advantage any longer of Anne's mistaken view of John, whom she believes to be carrying on a liaison with Matilda. He asks his father to have the situation explained to Anne as delicately as possible.

NOTES AND GLOSSARY:
Hardy passes from high summer to the following spring in this chapter; he almost always ignores winter as symbolically unsuited to this story of young people choosing partners. The broad comedy of Mrs Loveday's encouragement of Festus is a contrast to Hardy's wry understanding of her motives of jealousy and disillusionment; something of his traditionally bleak view of marriage comes through even in this idyllic novel. The scene with the volunteers is Hardy's proof that the individual retains his distinct personality even when subordinated to military drill, since the inefficiency of the local soldiers springs from their rough but thorough sense of their independence. The threat of invasion prompts Anne to fall in love with the adoring Bob and Bob to clear his brother's name; the fear of war brings about a noticeable improvement in each character.

Frederick William's Patagonians: a warlike eighteenth-century King of Prussia had recruited exceptionally tall and violent soldiers from Patagonia in order to form his personal guard
Martinmas: 11 November
katridge: local pronunciation of 'cartridge'
benefit-club staves: countrymen and countrywomen paid money into 'benefit clubs' last century for the pleasure of a ritual walk, a feast and a dance at common expense; 'wands' or 'staves' were kept as marks of membership

Chapter 24: A Letter, a Visitor, and a Tin Box

Once Anne knows John's real motives, she weeps in pity for him and writes an impulsive letter begging his forgiveness. Old Derriman bribes Anne with sweetmeats to come to the Hall and take responsibility for his precious box; he believes that when the French invade England, only the women will be spared. He buries his treasure in the cellars and gives Anne a paper with the directions for finding it, which she memorises.

NOTES AND GLOSSARY:
Anne behaves with a refreshing candour in writing so impetuously to her former suitor. Old Derriman's 'courting' of Anne with gifts parodies the behaviour of her three real lovers, but he can face the death or injury of Anne without a qualm, and his pathetic selfishness is a warning of what people become without human ties to soften them.

you bain't: a local form of 'you aren't'

Chapter 25: Festus shows his Love

On his way to the Hall to get money, Festus meets Matilda, now engaged as an actress at the Budmouth theatre, and they flatter each other cynically. He abandons her when Anne approaches, and feigns a seizure to bring the girl to his side; when she realises this is a scheme for a kiss, she runs away and Festus overbalances into a stream when he tries to follow her. Anne's tenderness for the Loveday men increases as the danger of invasion grows. She finds she has lost Derriman's paper and writes a duplicate; the careful Matilda has found and pocketed the original.

NOTES AND GLOSSARY:
Matilda's inner thoughts are rarely recorded, but her sauntering about the neighbourhood suggests that she is brooding resentfully about Bob's neglect of her. Her meeting with Festus shows each playing up to the vanity of the other and prepares us for the suddenness of their marriage at the end of the novel. Anne's flight from Festus is a rehearsal for her more serious peril in Chapter 27, and his feigning of a heart seizure foreshadows the real death of his uncle and coarsely burlesques the mortal peril in which John stands. Anne's sudden sympathy for him shows that her emotions are most deeply stirred when her pity is aroused, and at a more serious level, that our sense of our own mortality prompts us to strengthen our claim on life by falling in love. Festus is tossed in the river as much for mocking these life-and-death issues as for pestering Anne. While Anne and her mother have their petty snobbery chastened by their need for the Loveday men in this emergency, Maltilda

is untouched by the worries of respectable women and property-owners, and saunters back to Budmouth, living only for the day.

apoplexy: heart-failure
Paul-and-Virginia life: a reference to the famous novel *Paul et Virginie*, 1787, by Bernardin de St-Pierre (1737–1814); it was an idyllic picture of romantic love and had a formative influence on the young Hardy

---

Chapter 26: The Alarm

The beacon flare goes up to signal the landing of Napoleon's army, and the Loveday men set off as volunteers while the women take the gig to a relative's house farther inland. Festus decides that love has a higher claim on him than military glory and sets out to hide with Anne, but his own cavalrymen block his cowardly escape. When he hears from a passing officer that the beacon was lit in error, he shows true valour at last, ridiculing the natural fears of his comrades as soon as he catches up with them, and galloping off just before they can give him the punishment he deserves.

NOTES AND GLOSSARY:
Although the invasion scare quite reasonably excites the characters in the novel, we know that Napoleon never did invade England, and the interest of the chapter lies in the typical responses of the characters to the emergency. When Festus taunts his fellow-soldiers we feel a strong impatience with him, as we had not patronised the grief of the Loveday household as it dispersed to war or exile. Hardy insists on the need to treat the small disasters and triumphs of his ordinary characters with grave sympathy, and Festus in his oafishness mocks this seriousness.

the days of Noe: a biblical phrase, implying the carelessness of a nation living just before general destruction
wales: the planks forming the sides of a wooden ship
Minden: a battle of 1759, long before the present campaign
Ionic columns: the supports of a classical Greek temple
bagnet: the Miller's own form of 'bayonet'
sojer: an unlearned form of 'soldier'
frog-eating-Frenchmen: Englishmen traditionally despised the French for eating frogs as a table delicacy
thread-the-needle: a boisterous country dance

Chapter 27: Danger to Anne

Festus sends Bob off in the wrong direction so that he can give Anne the good news himself. The women have had an unlucky journey; an accident to the gig has left Anne to stay by herself to recover from her fright in a deserted cottage. She bolts the house against Festus and will not let him in to 'protect' her, and not even his proposal of marriage will make her unbolt the door. Festus, inflamed by rage and mortification, insists that he will break in and take 'forty kisses' by force, smashing his sword in comic rage on the shutters.

NOTES AND GLOSSARY:
Despite our foreknowledge that the invasion is a false alarm, we share the disquiet of Anne and the others as the landscape changes from the green shades of the Mill to sinister open country and mounds of glaring chalk. The action becomes more and more dreamlike as the gig's wheel falls off in hypnotic slow motion and Anne is left in the deserted cottage. Festus's persistent attempts to enter and his obsession with his 'forty kisses' have the strange logic of a dream which is helping Anne to understand the demands of her passionate nature still hidden under her polite reserve.

the Ark: see the First Book of Samuel in the Bible
wamble: an expressive local word meaning 'to wobble'

Chapter 28: Anne does Wonders

Anne leaves the safety of the house while Festus is pretending to have gone away, and in terror at her likely capture, leaps upon his horse and gallops towards Oxwell Hall. By coincidence, John Loveday is able to stop her in time to prevent injury, and Anne faints in his arms. He kisses her, Anne murmurs Festus's name, and the whole story comes out. Festus consoles himself for his loss by drinking long at the tavern, and John, convinced by the indiscreet letter that he is now Anne's choice, slaps the squire like a child as he sulks in the dark. But as John goes confidently back to the Mill he sees Anne rush out to embrace the returning Bob, and makes up his mind to give her up. Festus, in his fuddled state, thinks he has been beaten by Bob.

NOTES AND GLOSSARY:
Like a house in a dream, the cottage is too flimsy to keep out an intruder and Anne flings herself on a horse she cannot ride, not resuming her normal, timid personality until she is kissed by her rescuer John. She discovers in this extremity that she is capable of resourcefulness and strong feeling and will take advantage of this change in herself by the end of the chapter, when she throws herself into Bob's arms, her old 'discretion' forgotten.

tole: entice
carbine: a short rifle

the form of a Latin cross: a cross in which the lower limb is longer than
                the others
nunc: an obsolete familiar form of 'uncle'
smut: a fungus disease
staddles: stone pillars supporting a hayrick
aqua-tinted: having the delicate tones of a water-colour painting

---

Chapter 29: A Dissembler

Bob realises that John loves Anne and offers to resign her to him; John,
knowing that Anne really loves Bob, is forced to invent a fictitious
sweetheart to explain his melancholy distraction, and pretends that it is a
Budmouth actress.

NOTES AND GLOSSARY:
John's persistence in an unhappy love is parodied by Festus who 'could
not love lightly and gaily', though the squire's 'earnest, cross-tempered
and ... savage' passion is rebuked by John's chivalrous silence. We are
less interested in John's transparently fictitious love for a pretty actress
than in Anne and Bob's willingness to believe so improbable a falsehood
for their own peace of mind.

transparencies: there was a mania at this period for pictures which
                    were made visible by shining a light through them
up to the gunnel: (nautical slang) head over heels, completely
his suit don't fay: (*dialect*) his courting doesn't prosper

Chapter 30: At the Theatre Royal

John gets tickets for the play, and is aghast to see Matilda on the stage.
He decides it will not hurt for Anne and Bob to believe that she is his
choice after all, but Matilda assumes that Bob is present with Anne in
order to slight her. Festus, too, has a score to settle with Bob after the
beating in the tavern, and squire and actress agree to have a press-gang
carry Bob off to forced service in the navy. Matilda immediately regrets
her mean action.

NOTES AND GLOSSARY:
For a moment we see all the characters for what they are: actors in a brief
drama, and a farce at that, played against a backcloth of national
history. Everyone is at cross purposes and the self-deception and false
bearing of those in the audience match the complicated action of
Matilda and her troupe on stage. We see the difference between Festus
and Matilda in her rapid self-disgust after she has suggested vengeance
to Festus, while Festus nastily promises the sergeant that he can trap not

only Bob at Overcombe but other village lads as well. As a local squire, Festus should seek to protect the villagers and not trade them as a kind of slave in a private quarrel.

dog-days:	the hottest days of the year (from a Latin phrase meaning that the Dog-star rises with the sun)
piquet:	a small body of men left on guard
press-gang:	a notorious method of forced recruiting by which able-bodied men were kidnapped and carried aboard ship
frigate:	a three-masted warship, capable of speed
sea-legs:	the traditional rolling gait of a sailor

Chapter 31: Midnight Visitors

Bob is warned of the gang by a servant at the Budmouth inn. When the soldiers appear unexpectedly at the Mill itself, following Festus's instructions, Bob makes a daring escape and the intelligent Anne sends the party off on the wrong trail.

NOTES AND GLOSSARY:
For the past two chapters we have not seen Bob to advantage, as he has used John's generosity carelessly and has been appearing as a naive provincial dandy with assumed genteel manners. Hardy now lets us see his private thoughts and we understand the difficulties he is having with his conscience as the claims of Anne, his father and his country strive to be reconciled. The press-gang seems superficially to provide a mere dash of historical colour, but at a deeper level it illustrates Bob's need to find an authentic reason for his actions. As soon as he has proved his freedom as an individual by escaping the soldiers, he volunteers to fight beside them. The melodramatic actions of the novel always force a character to self-knowledge, so that however bizarre the events of the plot, the story is always psychologically believable.

pea-jacket:	a short woollen overcoat worn by sailors
cock-o'-wax:	a sarcastic term applied to Bob's outrageously fashionable dress
blow-hard:	a noisy but ineffectual person
cat-head:	a beam to which grain-sacks are hoisted

Chapter 32: Deliverance

A sympathetic soldier warns Anne that the troop will be back, and at daybreak she finds an exhausted Matilda who has walked from Budmouth to warn Bob. Together they find him lying in a drugged sleep in the garden, and as the soldiers are heard returning Matilda gets Anne to carry their intended victim under a bridge and out of sight. She kisses him gently, despite Anne's jealousy, and asks Anne to tell him of his real rescuer after their wedding. Bob explains that he has chewed poppy-heads, a powerful narcotic, to relieve the pain of the wound he got in escaping.

NOTES:
There is a magical quality to this chapter, as though nature, sympathetic to the anxiety of those at the Mill, has stopped the flight of time. The mill-wheel has ceased to turn, the landscape is eerily still, colour has not yet animated it, and the footprints of the soldiers remain in the dust on the bridge. Bob is discovered in the garden, fast asleep like the enchanted prince in a fairytale, his drugged indifference mimicking that forgetful-ness of Anne caused by his 'land-mermaids'. The dreamlike escape from the shepherd's cottage is re-enacted here as the women hide under the flimsy bridge, and the characters of the female rivals are developed neatly in their reactions to the kiss Matilda gives her former suitor, which itself parallels John's kissing of the unconscious Anne in Chapter 28. Matilda is right to rebuke Anne, as her embrace was a generous and forgiving gesture which laid no claim on a man who had rejected her rather shabbily.

Chapter 33: A Discovery turns the Scale

Bob can no longer be prevented from returning to sea, and he understands now that John has sacrificed his own chances with Anne for his younger brother's happiness. He salves his conscience by going to ask the famous Captain Hardy for a place on his ship the *Victory*, and makes a rapid departure, leaving the Mill in consternation.

NOTES AND GLOSSARY:
Anne's attempts to keep Bob at the Mill show her adopting innocently the methods of a Matilda. John's concern over the lock of hair which he believes to be Anne's recalls the lock of Bob's that Anne had burnt, and reminds us that John will find it difficult to overcome her love for the volatile sailor. The episode with Captain Hardy introduces the second of the personages from 'real' history and allows the fictional Bob to play his part in actual events. Hardy believed that Nelson's second-in-command was a distant relative; he could see the monument to Captain Hardy from his cottage at Bockhampton. Certainly, the mouth 'whose corners played between humour and grimness' suggests the novelist's own distinctive sense of irony. Captain Hardy is the authentic Hardy hero, sure of his place in history, mapping out his life with authority, faithful to his birthplace and family, and the active and skilled follower of a

useful profession. Bob's admiration of such a man raises the sailor-miller in our estimation. We notice that the Captain owns a 'dark little picture' painted by Anne's dead father; this provides a further link with the past and a suggestion of how life may be preserved in some sense through art.

bathing-machine:	the polite ranks of society entered the water from wheeled huts drawn into the sea by horses
curricle:	a light, two-wheeled private carriage of this period
skylarking:	deliberately dangerous displays of skill high in the rigging of a ship
grog:	a sailor's drink of hot water and rum
penetralia:	the innermost recesses of a temple which only the priest may enter
royals:	a small sail at the very top of a ship's mast

Chapter 34: A Speck on the Sea

As a parting gesture, Bob offers Anne to his more worthy brother. John refuses to accept this generosity, and keeps Anne loyally informed of the *Victory*'s movements, encouraging her to make a secret journey to Portland Beal to see the last of the warship, and joining in her fervent prayers for Bob's safety. In a lane near Budmouth Anne is discovered weeping by the King and his physician who are taking the waters at a medicinal spring. They ask kindly after her lover going off to war, and Anne wonders if this strange encounter will lead to a promotion for Bob.

NOTES AND GLOSSARY:
This chapter has a serious claim to be the finest in the novel. Anne has already come to terms with those human desires which place her on a level with socially inferior but equally vital characters, and now her grief at Bob's departure softens her haughtiness and teaches her patience. In the impressive passage describing the *Victory* sailing from Portland Beal, Hardy manipulates points of view so as to show us how differently the same scene may appear to separate observers, and that all varieties of feeling are worth recording. Anne watches in company with an old sailor who is seeing his own son go off to war, and her private grief is tenderly submerged in her sympathetic wish to interpret the scene for the old man as she sees it first through her own eyes and then through his telescope. Hardy uses precise yet poetic language as Anne sees the ship as an extension of the natural world: 'a leaf upon a tree', 'a bat', 'an egg' and 'a dead fly's wing upon a sheet of spider's web' suggest the fragility of the 'floating city' rather than its military might. The quotation from the Bible that she shares with John links their emotion here with myriads of other sorrowful farewells, and in the meeting with the King Anne has her own brush with history. Though her lover has just gone off to a frightful

conflict, his sovereign is ironically discussing the medicinal spring. The symbol of the healing water makes us remember that nature in this novel at least is benign, and that a special providence watches over Anne and Bob.

bollard:	a stout post to which ships are moored
beating up:	(obsolete in this sense) recruiting
coup d'oeil:	(*French*) as much as the eye can take in at a glance
lerret:	a small local boat built to withstand rough seas

Chapter 35: A Sailor enters

The family hears of the great battle off Cape Trafalgar and of the death of Admiral Nelson. No news comes of Bob, but that December a sailor from the *Victory* arrives with a story that Bob is still alive and engaged to marry a Portsmouth girl. Anne feigns indifference, but when her mother and John find her later in a dead faint, John condemns Bob as a 'worthless blockhead'.

NOTES AND GLOSSARY:
Hardy could have made Bob die at Trafalgar, leaving the field clear for John, so we share Anne's ignorance at this point. The chapter is uncharacteristically set in a snowy December, signifying bad news and a setback in the central love story; Anne's defiant singing when she hears of Bob's faithlessness echoes her similar song in Chapter 14, but the emotion is stronger this time as Anne now has feelings to be touched. Though we approve of John's bitter denunciation of his brother, the more experienced Miller reminds us of a general human frailty; Bob's neglect of Anne is no worse than Admiral Nelson's own notorious love-affair with a nobleman's wife, and conquerors as great as Nelson or as little as Bob need 'a little liberty allowed 'em.' He is not arguing for promiscuity, but assures us tolerantly that we cannot expect everyone to be as honourable as John.

hartshorn:	ammonia used by ladies to revive them in fainting-fits

Chapter 36: Derriman sees Chances

Festus, hearing of Bob's disloyalty, approaches Mrs Loveday for permission to propose to Anne. The mother lets slip that John is in love with Matilda, and Festus in his hatred of the trumpet-major feels a sudden passion for the actress. John tells Festus roundly that it was he who boxed his ears, and Festus manages to escape from the duel that John is forcing on him by claiming that the Miller's son is too low-born to issue a challenge. Festus courts Matilda in revenge, and as she is between theatrical engagements and between lovers, she encourages him. When she proves to have old Derriman's paper giving the hiding-place of the treasure, she is a more valuable prize than ever.

NOTES AND GLOSSARY:
Festus's latest application for Anne is the briefest yet, and his rapid favouring of Matilda is the natural coming-together of two cynical outcasts. But Matilda is a great deal more likeable, with a pleasantly wry sense of her own much-needed ability to carve out her own way in the world. It is interesting to see that Hardy treats duelling as a picturesque historical custom with no moralising on his part; novelists who wrote during the heyday of this illegal means of settling quarrels between gentlemen were usually impassioned opponents of the duel, and Hardy comes too late in the century for it to matter to him.

church verse: another reference to the Bible, 2 Samuel: 12, where King David has Uriah killed in order to possess his wife Bathsheba

how to take the current when it served: a reference to Shakespeare's *Julius Caesar*, Act IV, Scene 3

a stage where every man must play a part: Shakespeare's *The Merchant of Venice*, Act I, Scene 1

Chapter 37: Reaction

The Miller encourages John to woo Anne, but by late spring no answer has come to John's urgent letter asking his brother for leave to do so. John pleads his case: 'If you cannot love me, liking will be well enough.' Anne needs time to consider, but when John burns his hand badly in saving her from a scalding, she cannot hold out against him. The couple agree to go next day to see a figure of the King cut out from the chalk down, and just as he is looking forward to a rapid courtship, John gets a letter saying that Bob's latest love affair has not prospered and that he is coming back to Anne.

NOTES AND GLOSSARY:
We can see Anne's acceptance of John as an echo of Matilda's calculated engagement to Festus in the previous chapter; her reason tells her that this is her best chance of a husband and she is grateful for his attentions at such a low ebb in her emotional fortunes. This connection tends to put us on our guard against Anne's actions, and we gain no overwhelming sense of her happiness, despite the springlike setting. There are too many references to tears, and the pain caused to John's hand makes us wince. Although we are infuriated by the careless tone of Bob's letter, we are

not really convinced that John and Anne should marry; Anne is led to accept John by reason and gratitude, and the novel places instinct and romantic attraction above such prosaic values.

make-up: here, in the sense of 'make-believe'

Chapter 38: A Delicate Situation

Anne is perplexed and humiliated by John's respectfully distant manner and his encouraging talk of Bob, who has been promoted to the rank of lieutenant and will be the 'gentleman' Anne desires for a husband. At the site of an ancient church, Anne forces from John the admission of his self-sacrifice, and perversely feels a kind of love for the trumpet-major for the first time. John sends off a second letter to Bob; another suitor means to have Anne if he does not come home at once!

NOTES AND GLOSSARY:
Despite our preoccupation with John's tragi-comic predicament, a series of witty symbols keeps us in touch with the main themes of the novel. The characters literally walk through history as they traverse the gigantic figure of the King cut out from the downs in an absurd act of local patriotism, while Anne's complaints of dirty shoes are really her protest against John's sense of right and wrong ruining a deliciously romantic courtship. Her provocative teasing of the trumpet-major shows a new and playful Anne, a decided improvement on the pattern of ladylike behaviour in the early chapters, and her flirtatiousness is delicately balanced by the tender scene at the ruined church, symbolic of John's failure to get Anne to marry him and, in a larger sense, of the ravages of time. Anne's irrational attraction to John after his confession is Hardy's pointed demonstration of the perversity of romantic love, which cannot be denied or repressed for all that.

clipse: clasp in an embrace
rowel: the spiked wheel at the end of a spur
the organ of comparison ...: Hardy's jocular reference to the discredited 'science' of phrenology, or the diagnosing of character by the protuberances of the skull
chancel: the space about the altar where those about to be married stand with the priest
to be like St Paul: to be unmarried, like a priest of the Roman church who has taken vows of celibacy

---
Chapter 39: Bob Loveday struts up and down

Bob swears that he will reform, but the offended Anne holds out against his gifts and talk. Nevertheless, after four days she is speaking to the handsome officer, and their quarrel is almost ended during a berry-picking expedition. That evening Bob embraces Anne under cover of darkness at a fireworks display.

NOTES AND GLOSSARY:
Hardy suggests quietly that John's rank is really superior to Bob's, but Anne is not logical about such matters. Bob is reinstated in her affections in a comically speeded-up version of his return to favour after Matilda had left. The charming scene with the elderberries links the lovers with the hospitality of the Mill in the symbol of the wine-making, and shows them in a setting of natural beauty, swinging apart and together through the trees in a dancelike motion suggestive of their courtship. The embrace during the fireworks is a discreet acknowledgement of their passion for each other, which Hardy approves of as completely natural, and Anne's responsiveness here is an improvement on her coolly flirtatious wish to awaken John's ardour in the previous chapter. The brief but serious quarrel at the end of this chapter at last equates Anne's nature with the Mill itself, as her emotions make themselves a 'sluice' or waterway, and her tears flow like the millstream. She does right, it seems, to accept the brother who will not take her from her natural home.

epaulettes:	heavy shoulder ornaments of the officer class, originally worn to ward off sword-blows, then as badges of rank
the two Dromios:	comical identical twin servants in Shakespeare's *The Comedy of Errors*, never on stage together
slip-shod:	here in its original sense of 'wearing slippers'; now meaning 'slovenly' or 'careless'

Chapter 40: A Call on Business

A lovers' quarrel is interrupted by old Derriman with his box; Festus and Matilda have been searching for the treasure. Bob has struck up a sudden friendship with Festus who has told him tales of a wicked uncle and a 'hussy' who had jilted him; as Bob entertains the squire in the sitting room, old Derriman creeps in to steal back his box and a general scuffle ensues. Bob gives up his 'friend' and old Derriman is discovered next morning in a field, dead of heart failure. The box is found months later, hidden in Anne's own room without her knowledge, and the will makes her heiress of Oxwell Hall while the greedy Festus gets only enough to keep him decently.

NOTES AND GLOSSARY:
Anne has nothing to fear from Festus's stories, though in more tragically-inclined Hardy novels heroines have been driven to suicide by such revelations. Old Derriman's death is unemotionally described,

since death awaits all the characters in the novel and is only saddening, not terrifying. Anne's wish for both social position and independence is gratified when she becomes lady of the manor without having had to marry Festus; Hardy seems to be rewarding her for her progress to self-knowledge and her learning of a sympathetic kindness as a result of her own slight misfortunes.

put: a card-game
freehold: owned outright, so that the entire rents come to Festus

---

Chapter 41: John marches into the Night

John is unwilling to intrude upon the happiness of Anne and Bob, but he comes to a farewell supper given by the Miller, a shadow of the 'randy' where he had met Anne. Matilda and Festus are married, and Matilda gives John a sly wink as he passes the church. Though the soldiers are wished a quick victory and a safe return, Hardy lets us know that most of their number, including John, will perish in the campaign. John and Anne take a last farewell: 'Gratitude is not love', Anne explains tenderly as Bob boasts of his happiness. John goes out of the door and off to his death.

NOTES AND GLOSSARY:
Matilda and Festus, in their cynical union, comment ironically on John's idealism which has separated him from Anne. Hardy leaves us most impressed by the desperate common sense of Anne's last words to John, rather than the forced gaiety of the trumpet-major or the bumptious hilarity of the lucky Bob. Anne's final choice seems right for her, but her inevitable rejection of the 'better' man she cannot love is exquisitely sad. In the final, justly famous paragraph, John, lit only by the wavering flame of his father's candle, finally plunges into complete darkness where first the 'ring of his smart step' and then even his trumpet-call are 'silenced forever'. The snuffing out of this one life reminds us poignantly of our own mortality.

esprit de corps: (*French*) comradely spirit
Mulotters: mulattoes, or women of mixed race

Part 3

Commentary

The Trumpet-Major and its themes

The Trumpet-Major is an outwardly simple and innocent tale, an exercise in romance and apparent optimism by a novelist who came to write increasingly sombre fictions in which he proved the impossibility of human happiness in a world ruled by chance and the unforgiving laws of natural survival. It may surprise us, then, to find here a villain whose schemes always go astray, and a trio of main characters who are scarcely more complicated than children at play. Despite the general setting of a Europe at war, the military trappings are decorative rather than ominous: 'Here's a fine sight!' cries Anne at the beginning of the story, adding 'What does it mean?' only as an afterthought. We see that the novel is constructed around the false climax of the invasion which never takes place, and the historical climax of Trafalgar happens well off-stage, even if Bob Loveday does participate in it. Nor do the inner lives of the characters, as in novels by Jane Austen or George Eliot, compensate for the uneventfulness and provincialism of their existence; the Lovedays and the Garlands are not given to enquiring at all deeply into their motives or feelings. We suspect that Hardy may be criticising the increasingly articulate and analytical heroes and heroines of the nineteenth-century novel, and countering this tendency to sophistication by inventing people who act by instinct rather than intellect. Only John Loveday manages to rise above the unpretending level of Overcombe culture, and he is seen as a pale, thoughtful and often unhappy figure who seems to have strayed in from a more conventional novel. Yet his habit of questioning challenges the self-satisfaction of his birthplace, just as Matilda's role in the novel is to remind us that her world of stage illusion and commercial sexuality proves the innocence of the Mill a rare and precious commodity.

It may seem strange that Hardy has constructed a continually pleasing novel around the deliberately thin story of Anne Garland and her three lovers, which is only slightly fleshed out by the sub-plots of the bragging soldier-squire Festus, Matilda Johnson's attempts to live down her immoral past and find security and a husband, and the marriage of Anne's mother to a thriving miller. The reason that we are never dissatisfied with the airiness of the plot lies mainly in the richness of description with which Hardy surrounds his unambitious narrative, and the piquant contrasting of the characters' guilelessness with Hardy's own experienced, ironic vision. This is established not only through some famous authorial interventions but also through a constantly changing sense of scale and point of view. Hardy will frequently enter his characters' thoughts and explain their feelings and motives with a subtlety they could never manage, giving us a sympathetic sense of their predicaments, or he will invite us out of the protected, idyllic and somewhat limited world of Overcombe and show us the entire sweep of the downs and the coast, exhibiting his men and women as the charming and vain Lilliputians of Jonathan Swift, who created a race of tiny mortals mimicking the social, political and military foolishness of his contemporaries in *Gulliver's Travels* (1726). We are given an ironic perspective on the events of the story which the characters can never have, and this is underscored by Hardy's insistence that these beautiful, healthy, innocent men and women are all handfuls of grave-dust by the time we read their history.

Hardy uses his central story and its sub-plots as a means of exploring themes of permanent and disquieting interest; for example, his own preoccupation with time and mortality, the tragi-comic effects of romantic love, the place of short-lived man in the eternal world of nature, and the balance that must be struck between the individual with his private feelings and the citizen who is part of a demanding society. These themes, which foreshadow the main issues of the later tragic novels, are dealt with lightly here, but their presence warns us not to take the narrative at a trivial level.

The Greek philosopher Aristotle (384–322 BC) once remarked that 'the unreflective life is not worth living', and nineteenth-century novelists in general took him at his word, inventing characters who are enviably articulate about their inner lives and social roles. Hardy chooses to go against this tradition and writes with affection and without disrespect of people who have good principles without a moral philosophy, and whose merit lies in their calm enjoyment of the natural world. In his later novels, Hardy was to argue that nature was indifferent to man, though this translated itself in his art into an apparent hostility to human hopes rather than accidental benevolence. We find Hardy to be an emotional rather than a strictly logical creative artist. In this novel we see the outlines of tragedy shaping themselves in Anne's capriciousness and the rival claims of instinct and honour which torment John. But there is also a feeling of qualified optimism rare in Hardy, a sense of a special providence watching over Anne and Bob at least, because of their childlike joy in a native landscape rich in memory and natural beauty. The lovers inhabit a world long past for Hardy, simpler and more idyllic than the partly mechanised society which finds out the weaknesses of the later heroes and heroines. But Hardy also stands a little aside from the simplicity of Anne and Bob; his novel explores the tension between *innocence* and *experience*, the first shown in the almost magically protected Mill, and the second in the more sophisticated perspective of John and Matilda who have had to live by their own wits and whose professions place them at risk of death or infamy.

What, then, are Hardy's main concerns in this novel? A partial list should include:

The theme of time and mortality

This is demonstrated by the continual placing of short-lived man against the world of nature, where the often-mentioned insects exist still more briefly, and where the stars, the sea and the chalk of the downs continue unchanged. The symbolism of change and mortality may be quite open, as in the mill-stream itself 'stealing away like Time' in the first chapter, and the wornout millstones, worn-down stone stairs and the gentle, perpetual fall of flour-dust marking the imperceptible but destructive passing of the moment. Oxwell Hall, the occasion for one of Hardy's finest descriptions, is being reclaimed by the natural world on which it has imposed itself; once its noble owners have gone and the tenant-farmer Derriman inhabits it, rust, mushrooms and manure eat away at the fabric of the building and the broken sundial in the yard shows how decay is so complete that time has stopped. Old Derriman himself is depicted as a man for whom physical death will be almost irrelevant; he has cut himself off from all human ties in his greed for his treasure, and his face is hardly more than an animated skull.

At a more conventional level, the blossom Anne snatches up from the roadway shows her dimly recognising the shortness of her own life in the fragility of the flower, which is linked imaginatively to her own name of 'Garland'. Characters are mentioned who are already dead but live on through their possessions; Captain Hardy owns a 'dark little painting' which is all that we see of Anne's father, and the shadowy first Mrs Loveday lives on in the features of her second son and a collection of damaged china brought out to dignify his wedding.

The geometric design of the military camp mimics the constellations that shine above it, but the camp will disappear, leaving no mark on the downs. Soldiers pick ripe cherries, and Anne and Bob strip the elderberry boughs for wine, but the fruit is renewed by the endless seasonal cycle of nature while the human characters age, change and die. Death in the novel is shown only once, and then not violently, in the passing of old Derriman, though it is frequently asserted to be the common fate of man. Hardly assures us solemnly rather than ghoulishly that these people who claim our interest and affection are 'scattered about the world as military and other dust', and that history is indifferent to the individual. This is what a poet would recognise as the theme of *ubi sunt*: where are all past beauties gone? A poet also knows, as Hardy does, that our relishing of present delights depends on our awareness of their and our decline and death. Works as different as 'Ode on a Grecian Urn', by the Romantic poet John Keats (1795–1821), the more recent 'Sunday Morning', by the American poet Wallace Stevens (1879–1955), and the fairytale 'The Emperor's Nightingale', by the Danish storyteller Hans Christian Andersen (1805–75), prove the paradox that our sense of beauty is increased as we feel the nearness of change and decay.

The theme of the value of unregarded lives

Hardy assures us that this will be his subject when he chooses to write of a dramatic and decisive period in European history but sets in the foreground people with an unusually limited view of events. His philosophy here is an *egalitarian* one; he looks for similarity of motive between classes, and refuses to take note of differences of rank excepting that between creator and character. The egotism of Napoleon Bonaparte finds its village equivalent in the greed of the Derrimans, and the bravery and immoral life of Admiral Nelson has its counterpart, as the Miller hints, in the stout action and fickleness of Bob. The name of the Mill servant, David, hints at an even greater predecessor in the Bible who also sacrificed another man to his love for a woman, and whose sensuality in the midst of his greatness is usually interpreted as a symbol of our common sinfulness.

No character in the novel has an inner life to be ignored. The meanest illiterate servant has a right to wrap his bread and cheese in a newspaper describing the actions of the great. Shakespeare had made his sensitive philosopher Hamlet despair that the 'noble dust' of the conqueror Alexander might be traced to an earthenware plug for a wine-cask ('To what base uses may we come!'); though Hardy appreciates such irony, he does not see it here as a tragic statement of human ambition.

The English novel in the nineteenth century had made a point of treating the most ordinary lives with care and sympathy. In *Adam Bede*, 1859, and *Middlemarch*, 1871, George Eliot (1819–80) had insisted on the dignity of working people who brought a fine moral seriousness to their daily labour in insignificant rural parishes, while Elizabeth Gaskell (1870–65) gave a voice to the barely literate and depressed mill worker in the new industrial towns. Charles Dickens (1805–75) paid unpatronising attention to the family affections and awkwardly preserved self-respect of people living on the fringes of decent society or in desperate poverty. Social reporters such as Henry Mayhew (1812–87) interpreted the lives of labourers and complete outcasts, so that a middle-class reading public saw them as distinct individuals rather than a vague menace. As democracy became an inevitable political force in Britain the reading public sought to understand those depressed sections of society which were nevertheless to have a vote, and the novel in particular was marked by a concern for people at the meanest levels of society.

The problem of romantic love

The question every reader must settle is, of course, did Anne do right to marry Bob rather than the more likely suitor John? What does her choice represent? We have to decide whether Hardy is creating a minor tragedy of human wilfulness out of Anne's decision to marry the 'weathercock' rather than the man of honour—thus setting Anne beside a large collection of impetuous Hardy heroines who live to regret their choices—or whether Anne is marrying Bob because she has perceived his hidden merits and knows that he will compensate for a certain coldness in her character. Hardy does not make the judgement easy for us, since we are given a fair knowledge of the inner feelings of each brother and know that each has a right to Anne. There is a brief and touching emblem of the essentially three-fold relationship in Chapter 30, where 'Anne stood between the two brothers, who protectively joined their hands behind her back, as if she were a delicate piece of statuary that a push might damage.' Unfortunately the novel and social morality each demanded that Anne make a final choice, and Hardy uses the pressure for this decision to show that all happiness is purchased by someone else's pain, and that a satisfying life is a rare stroke of good fortune rather than the result of virtue. The final chapter of the novel must give us a qualm of discomfort as John goes off to die in Spain and Bob proves that he lacks the imagination to value his brother's sacrifice rightly.

Perhaps we can reach a solution to this difficult question if we think of the significance of *setting* in the novel. In choosing Bob, Anne is wedding herself to Overcombe and reaffirming her ties to home and family, just as in rejecting Matilda Bob had been responding to the claims of his childhood memories. Had Anne married John, she would have been condemned to the shiftless existence of a 'butterfly wife' seen in the second chapter, or to the perpetuation of her life as a daughter at the Mill while John served overseas. But even if we can make out a good case for Anne's decision, Hardy leaves us with a slightly sour view of marriage. Anne is embarrassed and excluded by her mother's acceptance of the Miller, and the new Mrs Loveday feels the bitterness of her diminished social position once the glamour of courtship has worn off. The novel remains a comedy only because Anne and Matilda go into their somewhat unsatisfactory marriages with a clear-eyed acceptance of their husbands' limitations and their own very good chances of making good a want of common sense in their men.

The ideal of romantic love has been a distinguishing feature of Western literature since its birth in the chivalric society of twelfth-century France, an aristocratic world dedicated, in its literature at least, to ideals of honour and self-sacrifice in the relationships between the sexes. From its beginnings as a theme, romantic love has usually inspired both the admiration and distrust of writers: a passion which overmasters reason is a compelling symbol of individualism, but a threat to any form of social order. Throughout his novels Hardy illustrates with ironic impartiality the irresistible force of wayward sexual attraction and the implacable hatred of society for such liaisons which, left to themselves, end in mutual or one-sided disgust. After the novels, his poems show the old unresolved tensions still fretting him; but here the feelings of romantic love are reserved for women who have died, and we are back where romantic love began, in the yearning for the unattainable.

It is worth considering whether Anne does not half deliberately redress an imbalance in her own life in marrying Bob. His enthusiastic and spontaneous approach to life appeals to her; in the opening chapters we see her faintly dissatisfied with the perfection of her ladylike behaviour and exclusive dignity. In matching her with the unintellectual but lively sailor, Hardy may be arguing the supremacy of natural instinct over social decorum, rather in the ways used later by the early twentieth-century novelists E.M. Forster (1879–1970) and D.H. Lawrence (1885–1930).

Hardy's view of nature

One of the reasons Hardy sets his novel back in the early years of the nineteenth century is to force his readers to look at the natural world in a fresh way. By 1880 the Romantic revolution in sensibility had worn itself down into inoffensive poetic conventionalities and the beginnings of an exclusive 'aestheticism' appealing only to the intellectually privileged. The original insistence of the Romantic poets Wordsworth (1770–1850) and Coleridge (1772–1834) that poetry rediscover the language of the common people and concern itself with their emotions was to some extent neglected. Hardy was the true heir of the founding Romantic poets in his awareness that nature must always be seen as if for the first time, and that the enjoyment of natural beauty involves our faculty of memory and a sense of time passing and experience gained. Nature, for all these poets, calls formal education into question while teaching us moral values which may go against the beliefs of society in general.

Hardy felt an impatience with lazy minds that merely filtered natural landscape through quotations from fashionable poetry, and writes satirically of Matilda's journey to the Mill:

> As Nature was hardly invented at this early point of the century, Bob's Matilda could not say much about the glamour of the hills, or the shimmering of the foliage, or the wealth of glory in the distant sea, as she would doubtless have done had she lived later on . . . . (Chapter 16)

Readers with a background in the period may object that the heroines of the novelist Jane Austen (1775–1817), contemporaries of Matilda and Anne, do habitually appreciate nature by reflecting on quotations from poets such as William Cowper (1731–1800) and Sir Walter Scott (1771–1832), but these ladies inhabit a higher level of society and a world where sophistication is much admired. Hardy's point stands; his characters have a truly innocent eye, and even the idiotic Festus, sublimely unresponsive to the joys of the intellect, can notice the 'giltycups' which colour Anne's stockings, while Anne and Bob take a childlike pleasure in the bounty that surrounds them, finally swinging like infants through the elder-bushes, in a perfect identification with the world of nature. John, the most subtle character in the novel, finds in nature the mirror to his own generally pessimistic and withdrawn reflections, as in the superb passage where Hardy allows him to watch every bubble and insect, symbolising his own brief life captured in the ray of light issuing from Anne's bedchamber.

The immense care Hardy takes in this novel over the descriptive passages, so that more often than not they impress us more than the characters (we know more about the Mill than its Miller, for example), suggests that people in the story are to be judged by the fullness of their response to the natural world, and that the fragility of human life is made up for in some way by the pleasure each generation takes in the same loveliness.

Hardy and the historical novel

In a simple sense, the nineteenth-century novel is frequently 'historical' in that it is set at a date somewhat earlier than the time of writing. Dickens (1812–70), Thackeray (1811–63), George Eliot (1819–80) and Charlotte (1816–55) and Emily Brontë (1818–48) set the greater part of their fiction in periods which recall either their own childhoods or eras in which the national character was altering in some critical way: *Middlemarch*, 1871, for example, deals with the rival claims of the individual and society and is set symbolically during the passage of the Reform Bill which was to enfranchise a larger section of the population. Dickens found that the description of vanished social abuses, like the Marshalsea Prison for debtors, provided him with almost poetic examples of human folly that transcended mere satire and made his novels apt commentaries on all possible states of society. Sir Walter Scott, whose Waverley Novels invented the historical novel as the English nineteenth century knew it, moved far beyond the simple exploitation of the picturesque into a dramatisation of conflicting states of mind within the individual or the national consciousness. His *Waverley*, 1814, is set at just such a remove from events as Hardy's less exciting *The Trumpet-Major*: just beyond the reach of living memory.

Why did the Napoleonic Wars in particular capture the imagination of so many writers? Stendhal [Henri Beyle] (1783–1842) produced *La Chartreuse de Parme (The Charterhouse of Parma)* in France in 1839, the English Thackeray had his *Vanity Fair* published in 1847, while *War and Peace*, the Russian classic of 1865–9 by Leo Tolstoy (1828–1910), has some claim to be the greatest novel of the century. The answer is complicated, but probably writers felt obliged to come to terms with the problem of egotism which Bonaparte posed; he had been both idolised and rejected by Europe, and while his energy and ambition captivated the imagination, there was something reassuring in the way that the forces of reaction, piety, and a homely distaste for glory had conspired to send him to exile and oblivion. Novels set in this period have evident differences but also some common ground. Tolstoy, on a much vaster canvas and with incomparably greater natural gifts than Hardy, also shows the fabric of a tightly-knit society resisting the invader, and the forces of continuity and unheroic domestic life succeeding where the uncommon individual's pessimism and scrupulous honour lead only to death. In *War and Peace* Natasha marries the reformed libertine Pierre, instead of the austere romantic hero Andrei, just as Anne marries Bob rather than John. Thackeray in *Vanity Fair* shows that the greed of Napoleon and a London merchant are basically the same, but he can modify his usual tone of comic distaste in order to turn his unintelligent characters into moving examples of the grieving woman and the heroic fallen soldier. In all these novels, the vastness of the war and the time that has elapsed since the conflict make the daily petty concerns of the characters all the more human and poignant.

The literary qualities of *The Trumpet-Major*

Hardy's prose style

Hardy's prose style is not usually regarded as a strong point in his novels; he was a self-taught writer, not always from the best models, and his most powerful works of imagination are often marred by pedantic expressions or intrusive quotations from other writers. Yet this comparatively minor novel is interestingly free from such faults: 'It would be superfluous to transcribe Bob's answer' is the only shabby sentence that springs to mind. The unreflectiveness of Hardy's characters saves them from the ponderous philosophising of his tragic heroes and heroines; when these people are deeply moved, as in Anne's farewell to the *Victory*, they have the Bible to express their emotion. Matilda uses stagey dialogue in her conversations with Festus, but she is after all an actress, and even here Hardy comments ironically on the main issue of the novel by having her borrow lines from a Shakespearian character who is sacrificing his life so that another man may have the woman of his choice. Bob's obsessive use of nautical slang may jar on the modern reader, but it helps remind us that men in this novel are judged by their competence in their professions. Conversations in the novel tend to be oblique rather than direct, with real wishes expressed sidelong through flirtation or gesture, changes of garments, or Hardy's own interpretation of his characters' feelings. There is a great deal of faintly comic constraint, as in Anne and John's talks across rows of vegetables, Matilda's muddled introduction of fresh subjects of conversation into her chatter when she meets the Garland ladies, and Anne's quaintly malicious teasing of the slow-witted Festus.

The spoken language of the characters in the novel has an appeal met only occasionally in other Hardy works. John's honourable feelings are sensitively undercut by his imperfect, countrified grammar which Anne has instinctively corrected in her own speech; our awareness of his little lapses makes him more human in our eyes. The Miller speaks little but always to the point, and his almost proverbial utterances establish the values of the community: Mrs Garland speaks in the first chapter of going to the Miller to 'hear what he thinks of it all,' and his comments that "Tis as well to be neighbourly with folks, if they be not quite onbearable' (Chapter 5) and 'folk might call thee a fool, and say thy brains were turning to water' (Chapter 22) show him putting both his sons in order. Bob calls upon instinctive rhetoric to defend his own easy-going philosophy against his brother's austere code of honour:

'You have made me miserable, and all for nothing. I tell you she was good enough for me; and as long as I knew nothing about what you say of her history, what difference would it have made to me? Never was there a young woman who was better company; and she loved a merry song as I do myself.' (Chapter 19)

That speech, and the Miller's unassuming reminiscence that he was five years a-courting his wife, show in their unpretentious gravity that all human feeling must be honoured in this novel, and not just the conventional morality of John and Anne. Hardy symbolises this by allowing the swearing of the Casterbridge coachman to exist alongside the preaching of the parson.

The great moments in this carefully crafted novel belong not to conversations nor even to descriptions of characters, but to the evocations of landscape: the Mill itself, Oxwell Hall, the review on the downs, the passing of the *Victory* over the horizon. Hardy's dense, pictorial style is carefully contrived to suggest nature forever renewing itself while the works of man decay, and the pathos of man's belief that his armies or his industry can make any lasting mark in a world where the massed troops of Napoleon appear to the distant eye as a silvery school of mackerel, and warships as 'black spiders suspended in the air'.

Plot and character development

Hardy's choice of an historical setting immediately limits his power to manoeuvre as a storyteller, and places him on an unusually equal footing with his readers. We know, as he did, that Napoleon never did invade England, and that the Loveday family's fears are unfounded. Consequently, what should be the climax of the novel—the flight from the Mill—does not engage our emotions very deeply. The action at Trafalgar involving Bob takes place 'off-stage', and by then our interest has been carefully re-invested in John Loveday, so that we cannot find a true climax here either. Hardy seems to be warning us not to look for the conventional excitements of a novel, and directs our attention away from events so that we can concentrate instead on the responses of his characters and his own attitude to the flight of time.

The Derrimans seem at first to promise a rich complication of plot, as Festus stands in the way of the brothers as a suitor for Anne and appears malicious enough to threaten a duel or other dangers for his rivals. Yet Anne is hardly tempted by the superior social standing of this 'cross baby' and her occasional toying with the idea of marrying him is usually designed to please or irritate her mother and gives her the chance to shift her affections from one brother to the other. Festus remains a pure buffoon with some good lines of dialogue to his credit, and he is the unwitting catalyst in Anne's discovery that she is not a prudish young miss but an affectionate and passionate woman. Festus's ridiculous passion for her awakens her dormant feelings for Bob. Old Derriman illustrates the virtues of family affection and generosity in the novel, since he possesses neither and is a pathetic, shrivelled old husk, existing only to give Anne the inheritance that makes her a truly independent lady at the end of the novel.

Only Anne shows a marked change of character, but this fixity is something we find comfortable rather than tiresome. John Loveday is still the schoolboy protector of Anne, with an ambition for art and music that will take him away from the limited world of Overcombe. His attitude to Bob was fixed forever when he cared for him as a child after the death of their mother. Festus is still the brawling, weeping bully he was as a boy, forever being put in his place by stronger women, and Bob is the impulsive, good-natured lad who ran into a burning house to save a child. Captain Hardy knew as a boy entering the navy what the pattern of his life would be and followed it faithfully. Hardy sees in this early formation of character not a deadening rural stupidity, but proof that good principles are established by childhood environment, and that no agents from a cynical outside world can shake this morality.

As in his later, tragic novels, Hardy allows minor characters to comment on the values of the central personages. Matilda is apparently a woman of bad character but she is in many ways like the innocent Anne; when Anne throws herself on Festus's horse to escape his advances or runs to drop Bob's hat at the crossroads to mislead the press-gang, she is as resourceful as the actress. When she attempts to keep Bob with her by the charms of her costume and song, she is using the methods Matilda employs to win protectors in a less idyllic world. Anne in no way forfeits our respect for this, but Hardy asks us to investigate our objections to Matilda.

Imagery and symbolism

Nothing in this novel is as important as Hardy's perfectly realised and intensely described visual imagery, which recalls a vanished age in sharp detail and in terms which the characters would not find foreign to their way of thinking. David's seed-cake 'opened to the knife like a speckled buttercup', ships are like 'black spiders' in the distance, one like 'an egg on end', a horse and gig are 'two specks the size of caraway seeds' on a distant road, coaches going to Budmouth like 'ants on an ant-walk', and Napoleon's army exercising at Boulogne like 'a school of mackerel' 'twinkling ... under the rays of the sun'. Characters crowding into the mill doorway to hear Bob's letter partially cover each other 'like a hand of cards'. At no point does Hardy exploit his superior learning or experience; he interprets a past world for us through the clear eyes of his rustic characters.

Hardy liked to have his early novels compared to paintings 'of the Dutch school', since he felt that, like the seventeenth-century Dutch and Flemish painters, he was depicting individuals of marked character moving in commonplace surroundings where every homely detail gained dignity from the painter's fastidious attention to its form and function. Here the simple gestures of daily life are not only recorded for their homely charm, but they serve to mark the passage of time which will destroy all the participants in the story. Mrs Garland shakes the crumbs from the breakfast tablecloth, the servant sets out cleaned dinner-plates for the cats to lick, Anne clinks coins into the Miller's hand in payment for their next ration of flour, and the Miller obsessively snuffs his candles before the fall of wax into the 'shrouds' of country superstition can prove how the evening of his party has stolen away. Bob, as we have seen, falls in love not only with Anne but with all the memories of acts of daily life which are summed up in her graces, while Anne marries him not only for his exuberance and affection, but because he will enable her to stay in a world she knows. The wandering life to which John invites her contains no loving repetition of familiar acts of hospitality and housekeeping; it is perilously close to that rootless existence which sums up the degradation of tragic figures like Jude and Tess.

Hardy turns away from the purely decorative historical detail in favour of the homely and familiar, concentrating on the amateurish patriotic displays of Budmouth, while the King himself appears as a simple, bluff gentleman, the 'Farmer George' of history, who passes the family in a dusty old leather coach. Mrs Garland easily reproduces the modest splendour of his Queen when she becomes Mrs Loveday. John's brilliant and at times inconveniently splendid uniform soon loses its exotic charm, for us as well as Anne, as we become more interested in the man rather than his clothing, and 'his gold lace, buckles and spurs lost all their strangeness and were as familiar to her as her own clothes.' (Chapter 10). The heroine's own garments are described less for their own sake than to convey a sense of English society at large; the draperies provided by a peddler, her holiday clothes only four years behind London fashion, and the real lace now no longer available to women of her social class, which produces one of Hardy's most enchanting visions of a vanished rural life:

> ... bought of the woman who travelled from that place to Overcombe and its neighbourhood with a basketful of her own manufacture, and a cushion on which she worked by the wayside. (Chapter 30)

The Miller himself is impervious to changes of fashion; his best coat, like his opinions, has lasted him for thirty years. Hardy does not exploit the exotic appeal of the period in a tasteless way; by degrees we come to ignore the outward differences between 1804 and our own day, as we concentrate on the permanent issues of human nature and emotion.

Hardy's metaphysic

The Trumpet-Major is not a novel of ideas, and indeed it chooses to prefer the unthinking, instinctual man or woman to the sensitive and reflective individual; or so we assume from Bob's marriage to Anne and John's exile and death. Characters are judged by their appreciation of the natural world and their closeness to it, by their capacity for feeling and enjoyment of life, and by their ability to take their place in the rural world to which they are born. There is a strong sense of the rightness of community life and the opinion of the majority, proved, for instance, in the villagers' critical response to the letter in which Bob announces his forthcoming marriage to Matilda. But Overcombe is generous in its judgements, and not even the despicable Festus and his miserable uncle are excluded from the simple pleasures of the village.

Nevertheless, Hardy cannot help showing a reverse side to this ideal picture of a countryside which had disappeared by 1880. Thoughtful men such as John outgrow Overcombe, and the experience and intelligence of the trumpet-major continually match themselves to the ironic vision of the novelist and question the unenquiring simplicity of Bob and the others. The novel would not enchant and move us as it does if we did not, like the readers of pastoral poetry, know that we are enjoying a vision of country life unreal in its perfection, over which the threat of change and death hovers ominously.

Hardy's novel is firmly egalitarian; the central moral of *The Trumpet-Major* is that no experience may be disregarded by the imaginative historian, and that human history is a gigantic accumulation of suffering, happiness, moments of blindness and sudden insights, and endless sense impressions by which the objective world is understood by separate individuals. The thoroughness of Hardy's evocation of different lives is his real achievement in this novel.

Hardy neither attacks nor defends religious orthodoxy in *The Trumpet-Major*. His characters are uniformly pious and are regular church-goers, though he observes acidly that the new obsession with Bonaparte has tended to overwhelm a more positive devotion. There are many hints that the villagers' virtues come not from their religious principles but from a strong sense of community, and their spirit is a doggedly secular one. 'I'd as soon see churches fall as good drink wasted,' says the Mill servant, and it is in the hospitable parties at the Mill, not in the church, that the values of the novel are most thoroughly upheld. The Mill stands as a symbol of community over four centuries, while the church at Faringdon has fallen into ruin.

While the changeless world of nature alternately charms us and gives us a desolating sense of the brevity of human life, Hardy manages to suggest something existing beyond the visible world. He takes care in his novels never to outline this vague presence too carefully; to analyse it would destroy its brooding power. But the carefully controlled plot and final coming together of the happy lovers seem to indicate a watchful and benign providence taking care of those people who are spontaneously close to the world of nature; the reverse of the malign and dangerous fate that overtakes the heroes and heroines of the last novels and which has its hand in the destruction of John Loveday.

The characters of *The Trumpet-Major*

Anne Garland

Anne is the only character to show a marked development during the novel, and we are pleasantly surprised to see the 'prim and stiff' beauty of the early chapters grow into a sensible, frank and well-judging woman. Hardy insists on her charming vulnerability while he is not absurdly indulgent towards her. She is not quite logical in her claims to gentility, since she is only a landscape-painter's daughter, nor in her social evaluation of Festus and his uncle who are quite low-born, and she is naive while presuming to judge much more experienced people like John Loveday. Hardy comments quite acidly on her invariably good opinion of herself, as well as on a readership which expected its heroines to be patterns of good breeding whatever their income: 'Anne, whose unquestionable gentility amid somewhat homely surroundings has been many times insisted on ...' (Chapter 38). Anne is incurably flirtatious, but completely innocent of sexual guile. She seeks only the admiration of men, and it is fortunate that she meets in Bob someone who can awaken her own warm feelings. A very similar personality, Sue Bridehead, was to ruin a man very like John Loveday in *Jude the Obscure*, by enticing him with no intention of sharing his physical passion.

Hardy emphasises the gentleness of Anne's character by comparing her to small and inoffensive creatures of the natural world: a 'doe', a 'ewe' and a 'mouse'. Such comparisons offset Anne's snobbery and personal vanity, which Hardy does not deal with too harshly. She is fond of dress because she is lovely, and we are reminded sadly that her charms are now coffin-dust. Her exclusiveness, leading to her refusal of John Loveday who is merely 'respectable', saves her from a marriage that would sever her from her home. By the time Anne aids the old sailor at Portland Beal she has set aside the finicking distaste for the 'lower orders' which had so annoyed the villagers.

Anne gains our respect for making use of the small amount of adversity she encounters in her sheltered life to develop a more independent and sympathetic character. She grieves when her mother's remarriage excludes the daughter from a protective relationship, and when Bob proves fickle, but she uses these setbacks to develop a new resilience and a firmness of purpose. Anne's conversations with Festus prove that there is 'a fair quantity of life and warmth' in this pattern of ladylike decorum. When she flings herself impetuously into Bob's arms after the invasion scare, she proves she has strong instincts, and when she firmly rejects the man she admires but cannot love, she proves that she has the courage to trust them.

John Loveday

John Loveday probably commands a general respect without demanding enough of the reader's sympathy to turn the novel into a tragedy of failed hopes. A careful reading of the novel may in fact show that Hardy is demonstrating that Anne and John are a mismatched couple, and the rejection of John does not prove the unfairness of things in general and romantic attraction in particular. While Anne and John are both serious, discreet and conventional, Anne rejects the soldier's proposal vehemently, as she does not want to limit her life to narrow caution and duty. She yearns instead for the impulsive and passionate Bob, who is permitted to act out in his raffish, masculine life those strong feelings denied to women. This seems the most likely way of explaining Anne's desperation in John's two proposal scenes; she is rejecting not so much the man and his social standing as the worshipful, over-serious view of herself he insists upon.

If John is finally not right for Anne, it does not mean that he has serious faults. He is admirably sensitive, and in many ways too good for the unreflective life of Overcombe which he has outgrown to the extent of sharing Hardy's own ironic view of the world. John has 'a pleasant twinkle of the eye which approached the satirical', and despite his infatuation with Anne he is not a disagreeably obsessed lover; he can claim and carry off a tenderness for 'a pretty play-actress'.

John is a true Hardy hero in his fondness for his birthplace, his eager self-education despite humble beginnings (his grammar is still shaky), a poetic spirit which shows itself in his creation of the Aeolian harp and his musical career, and an ability to imagine what other people are feeling. People trust him instinctively for his 'honest face' and those with something to hide, like Matilda, fear his judgement and obey his orders. He has 'good nature' and 'experience', and a nice sense of honour which Hardy sees as true gentility, which finally turns the plot in Bob's favour. But John does not wear his virtues solemnly, for he has some of Bob's impulsiveness in giving all the money he has to Matilda when he packs her off. He is an intriguing blend of guilelessness ('the simplest fellow alive,' says Bob impatiently) and sophistication: a combination which destroys all Hardy's tragic heroes. We shall meet John Loveday again in more ambitious novels as any one of a number of men of fine principles and generous compassion who lack the egotism necessary for survival.

Robert Loveday (Bob)

Bob Loveday seems destined to make us despise him, yet he wins Anne and most of us approve. He is described glowingly in terms of youth, health and good looks, his ready smile at his meeting with the villagers 'shaken into fragments and scattered promiscuously' like cake or rice at a wedding, in Hardy's anticipatory metaphor.

We find a good deal to object to in Bob, who is 'too easily impressed by new faces', as Anne puts it with ladylike understatement. But only John Loveday takes Bob's fickleness to heart, and Hardy, like the Miller, takes a relaxed view of his random love-affairs; after all, Admiral Nelson and King David in the Bible shared his peccadillos, and qualities of bravery, generosity and affection outweigh a tendency to follow one 'land-mermaid' after another. Bob has a magical vitality; he makes a feast, gives gifts, eats hugely, dresses brilliantly, and attracts women with the vigour of a prince in the kind of fanciful 'Eastern tale' which had been avidly enjoyed by English readers from the middle of the eighteenth century. He awakens in Anne feelings she cannot discover in herself for the worthy but prosaic John. Bob tries to be fair to his brother when he has Anne told the truth about Matilda, and he shows a spirited sense of honour when he escapes the press-gang as a freeborn Englishman is bound to do, but then signs up voluntarily.

Anne is able to delude herself into believing that Bob is that impossibility, a 'gentleman-tradesman', and that after his final return from the sea he outranks John, but it is her instinctive preference that guides her to her choice. Bob's last words in the novel prove that he lacks the subtlety of imagination to value John's sacrifice rightly, but they do not shake our faith in the good-natured vitality for which Anne is marrying him.

Festus Derriman

The third and last of Anne's suitors is designed by Hardy as a figure of fun and has troubled many critics, who see him as contrasting too grossly with the lyrical tone of the novel. Festus suffers from the gentle and innocent plot; he does not tempt Anne seriously as a husband, and the novel is too decorous for us to suspect him of offering her serious harm, even when he has her trapped in a lonely cottage. Festus's infatuation and its cure parody the main emotional events of the novel; neither he nor John can 'love lightly and gaily'. Successful wooers such as Bob evidently can, and the squire's rapid growth of interest in Matilda when he hears that she is the trumpet-major's choice comically parallels Anne's temporary fancy for John Loveday when she learns of his self-sacrifice. The good health and fine looks of the Garlands and Lovedays, necessary to make us feel the poignancy of ageing and death, are made almost monstrous in Festus's enormous size, voice, and infantile energy. He is a true *miles gloriosus*, the boastful but cowardly soldier found in all literature. We cannot take Festus seriously, and we may decide that he is made absurd so that we should know what to take gravely. In the end,

Festus is disposed of as a husband to the rehabilitated Matilda, and lightly censured for his greed and pretension by losing his uncle's inheritance to Anne.

Matilda Johnson

Matilda is a likeable character despite the disadvantages of her profession and her maturity. Overcombe respects innocence and good looks, and Matilda has lost the first and is losing the other when we meet her. While Hardy cannot condone her immoral life without alienating his original readers at least, he does call Overcombe attitudes into question by setting about her rehabilitation as soon as Bob has agreed to cast her off. John had known her by repute as a notorious camp-follower, but after her dismissal from the Mill Matilda advances her career smartly by getting a good engagement as an actress with a troupe of players fashionable enough to appear before royalty. By the end of the novel she is established as Anne's equal through her marriage to Festus. Hardy hints throughout that Anne and Matilda are more alike than Anne will ever guess; each has 'ever-changing emotional interests' and is instinctively clever at calling out the protective instinct in men. Matilda's wink at the departing John in the final chapter asks what is the point of his 'honour'; she is the only character who is as intelligent and as experienced as the trumpet-major, but she chooses to take life ironically rather than tragically, and has dedicated herself to success and survival.

Old Derriman (Uncle Benjy)

The miser is always a favourite figure of comedy, particularly when he holds the fortune of a pretty and marriageable girl in his gift. Old Derriman loves Anne as much as he will love anyone, and woos her after a fashion so that she will protect the treasure which he loves like a mistress. He keeps alive in our minds the theme of mortality, since his froglike, skeletal appearance, like Death in popular woodcuts, makes his actual death at the end of the novel a mere matter of form. He is the opposite of the generous and hospitable Miller.

Mrs Garland, later Mrs Loveday

Hardy is divided between indulgent affection for this 'easy-minded' and 'unambitious' woman with her inappropriately girlish ways, and disapproval when she avoids her obligations as Anne's mother by her constant silliness. She provides an interesting example of Hardy's gift for exploring the feelings of people who cannot put their emotions into words when he analyses her discontent following her marriage to the Miller, and when she tries to stop Anne marrying into the family out of a mixture of feminine jealousy and social ambition. Like Bob, she is a 'weathercock' of 'versatile' sentiments, and, as with Bob, a fortunate marriage enables her to behave sensibly. She suffers somewhat from Hardy's revision of her character between his original draft and the serial publication, in order to minimise the tension between mother and child. It is essential for Hardy's purposes in this novel that Mrs Garland should be a very slight influence on her daughter so that Anne may take full credit for improving her own character.

Miller Loveday

Miller Loveday says little, and is less thoroughly described than his Mill, but he is the authentic voice of Overcombe wisdom. His name suggests the clarity of his moral vision, and his measured, proverbial utterances set his family right when they are bent on going wrong. His hospitality forges ties between people in the community just as his trade provides them with bread, 'the blessed staff of life'. He is the central symbol of family affection and the link between the generations which in a sense defeats time. In his rejection of fashion, his experienced wisdom, and his desire that his sons should continue his trade, he is a living example of the virtues of the common folk Hardy is celebrating: 'full of importance to the country at large, and ramifying through the unwritten history of England.'

Part 4

Hints for study

A guide to reading the novel

As you read the novel, keep your pen in hand to underline passages which seem to illustrate Hardy's themes. Devote a page of your notebook to each main character, and keep a 'file' of those phrases or anecdotes Hardy uses to develop our knowledge of their personalities. This will help you to keep the 'ever-changing emotional interests' of the plot in focus, and give you fair grounds for coming to a decision about the rightness or otherwise of Anne's acceptance of Bob. Pay careful attention to those passages where Hardy is letting us know the secret thoughts of a character.

The main *themes* of the novel are easy to identify: the shadow of death and the sadness of time's passing, the dignity of even the simplest personality, the pleasures and dangers of romantic love, and the compromises that have to be made between the needs of the individual and the demands of society. Note down those events and authorial statements which seem to identify these issues.

Try to acquire a sense of the *shape* of the narrative. There is the false climax of the invasion scare, the historical climax 'off-stage' at Trafalgar, and the emotional climax as John is forced by his own concept of honour to give Anne up to his brother.

Notice the way Hardy has developed *parallel incidents* within the novel, with the second such event usually more intense than the first. Perhaps he is showing us how people learn from experience. Festus waylays Anne on two occasions, in the meadows and on the deserted down, and each time she is bolder in admitting her feelings for Bob when she has escaped. Bob jilts Anne twice, first in his engagement to Matilda, and then much more discreditably in his proposal to a baker's daughter in Portsmouth. There are two stolen kisses, as John embraces the unconscious Anne after her desperate ride and Matilda kisses the sleeping Bob under the bridge. John courts Anne on two separate occasions and almost wins her the second time. The action of the novel opens and closes with a festive supper at the Mill.

What is the function of *melodrama*, or violent, exciting action in the novel? Often it can be an admission of failure, particularly in a serial-writer, an attempt to encourage the reader's flagging interest in a not very exciting or plausible story. Perhaps we find here that the episodes involving Anne's escape from Festus, the press-gang, and the invasion scare itself place the central characters in situations of stress or unreality and forcibly teach them something about themselves and their world.

Hardy's use of *setting* will occupy a lot of your attention. There are obvious contrasts of scale, as sometimes the most minute insects, sometimes the whole south coast and English Channel are observed. The protected, idyllic Overcombe Mill obviously contrasts with the rawness of the chalk downs and the decaying Oxwell Hall. We are aware of changes made by the actions of man on nature: a ruined church, a village that has disappeared, a figure of the King cut into the downs, the mushroom city of the military camp. But nature ends by reclaiming what man builds, and all his armies and fleets are as puny as swarms of insects and schools of fish.

There is some mild *social satire* to claim your attention: the theme of Anne's snobbish disdain (not shared by Hardy) for the honest Lovedays, and the villagers' insistence that they are as good as the Garlands. Discover what you can about the Derrimans and their background, and the lost family who owned Oxwell Hall before them. Budmouth gives Hardy lots of opportunity to use his historical research in some very attractive comic descriptions, but Casterbridge gives him more scope for social satire in his treatment of Bob's Sunday afternoon spent waiting for Matilda.

Conflict in the novel seems minimal, despite the wartime setting and the triangular love relationship. Festus is no match for the Loveday brothers, and John is able to send Matilda packing after one steely exchange. We find a truer conflict in Hardy's matching of irreconcilable attitudes to life: John's unyielding sense of honour and Matilda's pragmatic sense of survival; John's experienced good sense and Bob's ability to ignore the lessons of his past mistakes; John's habit of reflecting on the results of his actions, and Bob's knack of living for the moment. Anne, who shares the characteristics of both brothers in her reflective reserve and her impetuous hidden feelings, has to choose between the attitudes to life represented by the serious John and the instinctual Bob.

As Hardy's *language* is one of the best features of the novel, check those passages which seem particularly witty, pithy or poetic. Matilda's arrival at the Mill should interest you; also the departure of the *Victory* and any of John's conversations with Anne.

Be aware all the time of the effect of Hardy's *irony*; his continual reminders that his characters have no sense of their own mortality, and that only he can see their actions in the larger context of human nature and human suffering. Note those passages where he makes us aware of the characters existing in history, or being poignantly unaware of what time has in store for them.

Key passages for quotation

(1) Though nobody seemed to be looking on but the few at the window and in the village street, there were, as a matter of fact, many eyes converging upon that military arrival in its high and conspicuous position, not to mention the glances of birds and other wild creatures. Men in distant gardens, women in orchards and at cottage-doors, shepherds on remote hills, turnip-hoers in blue-green enclosures miles away, captains with spy-glasses out at sea, were regarding the picture keenly. Those three or four thousand men of one machine-like movement, some of them swashbucklers by nature; others, doubtless, of a quiet shop-keeping disposition who had inadvertently got into uniform—all of them had arrived from nobody knew where, and hence were matter of great curiosity. They seemed to the mere eye to belong to a different order of beings from those who inhabited the valleys below. Apparently unconscious and careless of what all the world was doing elsehwere, they remained picturesquely engrossed in the business of making themselves a habitation on the isolated spot which they had chosen. (Chapter 1)

COMMENT: Hardy produces a set-piece of compelling charm, in which the miniature details of this bird's-eye view of the scene remind us of the paintings of the Flemish master Breughel (1525–69). Throughout the novel Hardy approaches his subject with the eye of a painter, using the metaphors of composition, vanishing-points, aqua-tints and so on, since it is only through a careful *visual* re-creation of a vanished life that the characters in their setting can be made vivid to us. The stress in this paragraph is on the tension between the private emotions of the individual man and the generalising tendency of military discipline or the 'mere eye' of the casual observer. Hardy has a characteristic respect for the individual and will show in this novel that history is actually a mosaic of separate, infinitely complex lives rather than a stage for heroes or a pattern of abstract events.

(2) The present writer, to whom this party has been described times out of number by members of the Loveday family and other aged people now passed away, can never enter the old living-room of Overcombe Mill without beholding the genial scene through the mists of the seventy or eighty years that intervene between then and now. First and brightest to the eye are the dozen candles, scattered about regardless of expense, and kept well snuffed by the Miller, who walks round the room at intervals of five minutes, snuffers in hand, and nips each wick with great precision, and with something of an executioner's grim look upon his face as he closes the snuffers

upon the neck of the candle. Next to the candle-light show the red and blue coats and white breeches of the solders—nearly twenty of them in all besides the ponderous Derriman—the head of the latter, and, indeed, the heads of all who are standing up, being in dangerous proximity to the black beams of the ceiling. There is not one among them who would attach any meaning to 'Vittoria,' or gather from the syllables 'Waterloo' the remotest idea of his own glory or death. (Chapter 5)

COMMENT: This is Hardy's most careful and formal statement of the theme of mortality within the novel, and he inserts himself into the narrative by claiming that he is writing a history from oral sources. He draws our attention first to himself in the present, 'seventy or eighty years' away from the events he is reviving in memory, and conjures them up with a painter's eye; first the sources of light and vitality in the candles, and then the areas of vivid colour. The Miller's obsession with candle-snuffing keeps us aware of the passing of time on the minutest scale as he makes his five-minute rounds of the room. 'Members of the Loveday family' hints that one of the sons must have married and had children. It is significant that the gentle parish history of the Lovedays and the universally known battle of Waterloo are given equal force by Hardy, and understandable in a novel dedicated to showing that all lives are of equal value.

(3) They [the downs] still spread their grassy surface to the sun as on that beautiful morning not, historically speaking, so very long ago; but the King and his fifteen thousand armed men, the horses, the bands of music, the princesses, the cream-coloured teams—the gorgeous centre-piece, in short, to which the downs were but the mere mount or margin—how entirely have they all passed and gone!—lying scattered about the world as military and other dust, some at Talavera, Albuera, Salamanca, Vittoria, Toulouse, and Waterloo; some in home churchyards; and a few small handfuls in royal vaults. (Chapter 12)

COMMENT: This quotation does in a more public and philosophical manner what Hardy had set about conveying through narrative in the former passage. He still uses the painter's eye, showing the scene like a painting in a frame, but the rhetoric soon takes over from the imagery in the roll-call of battle names. This passage owes something to Shakespeare's famous lines in *The Tempest* where the magician Prospero reflects on the artist's power to create the illusion of life:

Our revels now are ended. These our actors,
As I foretold you, were all spirits, and

Are melted into air, into thin air;
And, like the baseless fabric of this vision,
The cloud-capp'd towers, the gorgeous palaces,
The solemn temples, the great globe itself,
Yea, all which it inherit, shall dissolve,
And, like this insubstantial pageant faded,
Leave not a rack behind. We are such stuff
As dreams are made on, and our little life
Is rounded by a sleep.

(IV.1.146–58)

The message in Hardy's passage is that death comes to all men while nature remains unmoved; her permanent beauty both mocks us and consoles us.

(4) Anne had been adding up her little studies of the trumpet-major's character, and was surprised to find how the brightness of that character increased in her eyes with each examination. A kindly and gentle sensation was again aroused in her. Here was a neglected, heroic man, who, loving her to distraction, deliberately doomed himself to pensive shade to avoid even the appearance of standing in a brother's way. (Chapter 38)

COMMENT: With this passage, Hardy identifies Anne's careful and fair appraisal of John Loveday with our own sympathy for the hero of the novel, raising both characters in our estimation. Anne arrives at the level of understanding common to both author and reader, and we may detect a faint criticism in the way the honourable, introspective John 'dooms himself to pensive shade'. How far we take this negative suggestion depends on our view of the novel's meaning.

(5) Youth is foolish; and does a woman often let her reasoning in favour of the worthier stand in the way of her perverse desire for the less worthy at such times as these? (Chapter 40)

COMMENT: Hardy seems to be suggesting that Anne is making a wrong decision, but his interjection could be ironic; he could be admitting that reason has nothing to do with love, and that questions of sexual preference are decided at the level of instinct.

(6) The candle held by his father shed its waving light upon John's face and uniform as with a farewell smile he turned on the doorstone, backed by the black night; and in another moment he had plunged into the darkness, the ring of his smart step dying away upon the bridge as he joined his companions-in-arms, and went off to blow his trumpet till silenced for ever upon one of the bloody battle-fields of Spain. (Chapter 41)

COMMENT: This famous conclusion to the novel shows Hardy's assured use of visual imagery, particularly the play of light and shadow in the wavering of the candle-flame, suggesting a life to be snuffed out, and the final 'plunge' into complete darkness. Then we hear only sounds, until the brusque statement of John's death leaves us, as it were, sitting in a darkened theatre, reflecting on our own mortality.

Preparing for the examination

Your work for the examination begins when you first open a set text; always read with a pencil in your hand to note down any useful point that occurs to you. The well-prepared student does not waste time memorising successful essays or critical opinions, but comes to the examination with a mind well-stocked with impressions, phrases and character analyses that can be used as the specific questions require. No technique of preparation can equal a genuine interest in the works studied.

Obviously, consistent working throughout the year is more intelligent than nervous cramming at the last moment. Make a timetable for revision reading well in advance of the examination, check to see that you understand the criticisms your teacher has made of your written work, and read over the notes you have made in class. Practice in actual writing, preferably to the kind of time-limit you will have to face in the examination, is essential; you must make yourself fluent on paper and build up a varied stock of critical vocabulary you can call on in an examination. The habit of writing easily under pressure is especially necessary for students studying on their own, and should be practised constantly.

A student who has had practice in interpreting examination questions is likely to be a successful candidate. Look at previous examination papers whenever this is possible, to see the kinds of questions asked and the level of ability that is expected, even if the set texts are different. Again, this preparation is especially helpful for students working alone.

You will naturally take care to rest and to eat sensibly before the examination, so that you sit down to the paper in a calm and relaxed state of mind. Put your notes away a day or so before the examination, and read the texts themselves simply for enjoyment, so that their incidents are fresh in your mind.

The examination itself

Remember that your choice of questions and how you interpret their meaning is half the work of the examination. Take time to read the paper thoroughly, and be scrupulously careful about which and how many questions are to be answered. Circle or underline the instructions to be sure. Some students will start writing at once, but the promising candidate will take ten or fifteen minutes to think out the best approach to the topics chosen. It can be very damaging to your confidence to have to cross out a half-completed answer which you discover to be off the topic.

Decide as soon as you know the format of the paper how much time you can afford to spend on each of the questions. You should allow at least ten or fifteen minutes at the end of the examination for the revision of your answers as you allowed ten or fifteen minutes at the beginning for preparation. The time between should be divided intelligently; never let yourself go beyond the time you have allowed for a question, no matter how brilliantly you appear to be writing. The extra few marks that can be given for a remarkable performance will not make up for the disaster of a barely begun final question. Time spent revising answers is time well spent, and will prevent unpleasant worries as soon as the examination is over; you need to go back over the paper and correct those faults of spelling, expression and fact that everyone makes under the stress of examination. It goes without saying that a serious student will take advantage of all the time that is allotted for the examination, and not leave the room early.

The sensible student goes in to the examination with a mind well stocked with information, eager to see what questions will be asked, and prepared to answer the topics in an interested and original way.

Specimen examination answers

(1) Is *The Trumpet-Major* a tragedy or a comedy? Give your reasons.

At first reading, *The Trumpet-Major* seems to have most of the characteristics of a tragedy: the hero of the title is disappointed in his love for the attractive and intelligent heroine who prefers his somewhat spoiled and thoughtless brother, and he goes out to die on 'one of the bloody battle-fields of Spain.' John Loveday is more thoughtful and imaginative—more 'poetical' as Anne puts it—than the family and friends he left when he joined the army, and while everyone regards him with affection, no one except Anne is able to understand how exceptional he is. Hardy dwells on John's excellent qualities: his love for his soldier's life, his tender concern for Anne's welfare, his fondness for his childhood home, his taste for art in the creation of the Aeolian harp, and his exquisite sense of tact and honour in refusing to embarrass Anne by his presence when she rejects him and in declining to propose to her when Bob decides to come home. It seems hard that a man whose decency and kindliness result from his ready understanding of other people's feelings should end rejected and alone, and we feel a very real sadness at the close of the novel.

However, Bob, the lucky suitor, proves to have good points of his own. Anne is fascinated by his recklessness, his physical courage and vitality, and his amorous nature. At the beginning of the novel she seems somewhat tired of her 'correct' and reserved behaviour which condemns her to sit alone in her private rooms making copies of her father's paintings, and she is pleasantly impressed by the sailor's unceremonious treatment of her. While her conversations with John are always stilted and polite, Anne soon finds herself running to embrace Bob who calls up a warmth of feeling in her that she cannot discover for the 'better man', John. Hardy seems to be arguing that the warmth and openness of Bob's nature compensate Anne's original coldness and reserve which in fact attract the prudent and self-controlled John. John can only see the ladylike side of Anne, while Bob, for all his fickleness and limited intelligence, manages to awaken Anne's passionate nature.

Hardy surrounds Bob's final return to the Mill and the conclusion of the lovers' courtship with a wealth of symbols calculated to prove his sympathy with them: the shared chore of berry-picking to make the household wine, the firework display which suggests the strong and joyous emotions felt by Anne, and her tears which flow like the millstream itself as her old grievances are set aside. In addition, Anne's marriage to the sailor-turned-miller will keep her safe at Overcombe, in the natural world she knows so intimately, whereas marriage to John would have condemned her to the shiftless life of barracks and camps. In the face of the happiness of Anne and Bob, John wavers and fades in the candleflame held out by his father, and though we feel a natural grief for him, we are also satisfied that Anne is marrying the man who confirms her in her belief that she is a creature of passion as well as of reason.

The idyllic nature of the setting in the novel adds to our conviction that *The Trumpet-Major* is basically optimistic in its view of its central characters. The Mill is symbolically protected from the elements, just as Anne and her family understand little of human wickedness and have to face only the mildest of dramas in the false alarm of the invasion and Bob's silence after the battle of Trafalgar. We are given the impression that all the characters, excepting John, lead charmed lives, and that their histories are happy ones. None of the characters has changed very much from childhood, we are told, and at times we seem to be watching the games of infants, so innocent is the plot. Festus Derriman, the main comic presence in the novel, offers no real threat to Anne or the Loveday brothers, and his amusing and impotent rage as he smashes his sword on the shutters of Anne's refuge on the downs shows how little power the forces of evil have in this novel. A 'tragic' novel would be unlikely to contain such a buffoon as Festus, and the sources of real danger, such as the press-gang, the invasion scare, and Bob's duties on the *Victory*, would make us much more uneasy.

Despite the gentleness and optimism of Hardy's tale of unregarded lives, the novel, nevertheless, leaves us with a lingering sense of loss and the sadness of the human condition. All the characters are preoccupied with their own affairs and respond fully to the richness of the natural world and the excitements of history, and Hardy's recall of this vanished age in perfect detail down to the last insect and water-bubble is so meticulous that it is chilling to be reminded frequently by the author himself that all these healthy, lively and likeable characters are dead; John by the chances of war, and all the others through the inexorable passing of time. We value the characters and their sensory experience more because Hardy sets the charms of the natural world in the context of death; our own, as well as the characters' mortality.

The Trumpet-Major is not a tragedy in terms of its characterisation, since there is too much evidence that Anne makes the right decision in choosing Bob. But Hardy uses his conventionally beguiling story of country lovers to point out the brevity of human life and the vanity of our hopes for the future; Anne's loveliness, John's honour and Bob's ardour are swept away on the current of time as remorselessly as the warring armies of Europe.

---

(2) Analyse the use Hardy makes of the historical setting in *The Trumpet-Major*.

Hardy uses a momentous historical period but explores only trivial lives; he sets out to prove the value of the most ordinary individual who has as much capacity for feeling and suffering as a king or general. The parish history of Overcombe gets as much attention as the great victories of the period, because it is in details such as the pikes kept in the local church that the past is brought closer to the present. Hardy places his action just beyond living memory in order to impress us with his underlying theme of mortality. Finally, consider the question of *scale*; if the villagers are petty compared to the great wars of the decade, the armies and navies of the warring nations are mocked by a vast and eternal nature.

---

(3) 'Festus Derriman hardly seems to belong in *The Trumpet-Major*: he is a figure of farce who spoils the delicacy of the main love story.' Discuss.

If you choose to object to Festus, you will be in good critical company, and you will find good grounds in the novel for your argument. Be careful not to be too destructive in your criticism; it is always a wise policy in essays to look for the merits of a work rather than to 'tear it to pieces'. (On the other hand, don't be too gushing in your admiration.) Perhaps the delicacy of the love-triangle needs the hearty coarseness of Festus, and we could even argue that Anne turns in the end to Bob, who is part-way between the rather chilling deference of John and the vulgarity of the squire. Look back over the arguments in the preceding Notes suggesting that Festus unwittingly helps Anne to find qualities of daring and passion in herself. In addition, it may be a good thing that Festus is there to burlesque the adoration of the Loveday brothers, which could otherwise become a little too bloodless.

---

(4) Consider the role played by Matilda/Mrs Garland/old Derriman in the novel.

This question is usually a delight for the well-prepared student, and your personal file on each character can be pressed into service. In each case, you will be dealing with a *sub-plot*, and you must explain how it fits into the main action and how the minor character reflects at least one aspect of a central figure in the story. Try to include in your answer the quotations you have found which sum up the nature of the character.

---

(5) Show how Hardy uses natural imagery in *The Trumpet-Major*.

Again, your notes and marginal jottings will be of great value, and the choosing of useful examples is half the work of the answer. You will probably deal in detail with the descriptions of the Mill and Oxwell Hall, discuss the symbolism of the mill-stream and the cherry-picking, look at the way in which the landscape eventually reclaims the buildings imposed on it, and concentrate on showing throughout your essay that Hardy continually emphasises that nature is permanent while man's life is short. You should point out that Hardy makes us value his characters according to the strength of their response to the natural world, and the sensuous quality of his imagery is his way of reviving the dead past.

Part 5

Suggestions for further reading

The text

The best annotated edition of the text for students is the New Wessex Edition of *The Trumpet-Major*, Macmillan, London, 1974, which has an excellent introduction by Barbara Hardy. It contains Hardy's 1912 Preface, ample notes and glosses on dialect words, and a history of the text.

Criticism

The best critical text is J. I. M. Stewart's *Thomas Hardy: a critical biography*, Longman, London, 1971. The life of Hardy is considered in relation to his novels; an elegant, thought-provoking study which assesses other critics' opinions and forms a good introduction to the body of Hardy's work.

Biography

By far the best biography of Hardy is the recent two-volume study by Robert Gittings, *Young Thomas Hardy* and *The Older Hardy*, Heinemann, London, 1975 and 1978 respectively. It is also worth consulting *The Life of Thomas Hardy* by Hardy's second wife, Florence Emily Hardy. This curious book was actually written as a third-person autobiography by Hardy himself, and his wife added only four last chapters and a few corrections. This work was published originally as *The Early Life of Thomas Hardy*, Macmillan, London, 1928 and *The Later Years of Thomas Hardy*, Macmillan, London, 1930; they were published as a single volume by Macmillan, London, in 1962.

The author of these notes

MARGARET STONYK took her first degree at the University of Adelaide, South Australia, in 1967, and received her Ph.D. from the University of Leeds in 1970 for a thesis on William Morris and Victorian poetry. She has taught at universities in Australia and Canada, and was a lecturer at the University of Stirling in Scotland for three years. She has published articles on poetry and the fine arts in the nineteenth century and contributed a chapter to a volume of studies on Victorian poetry. Dr Stonyk is at work currently on a book surveying the art of biography, and is writing the volume on nineteenth-century English Literature in the new *Macmillan Histories of Literature*.

The first 250 titles

Series number